ROUTLEDGE LIBRARY EDITIONS: LITERARY THEORY

Volume 17

HISTORICAL CRITICISM AND THE MEANING OF TEXTS

HISTORICAL CRITICISM AND THE MEANING OF TEXTS

J. R. DE J. JACKSON

LONDON AND NEW YORK

First published in 1989 by Routledge

This edition first published in 2017
by Routledge
2 Park Square, Milton Park, Abingdon, Oxon OX14 4RN

and by Routledge
711 Third Avenue, New York, NY 10017

Routledge is an imprint of the Taylor & Francis Group, an informa business

© 1989 J. R. de J. Jackson

All rights reserved. No part of this book may be reprinted or reproduced or utilised in any form or by any electronic, mechanical, or other means, now known or hereafter invented, including photocopying and recording, or in any information storage or retrieval system, without permission in writing from the publishers.

Trademark notice: Product or corporate names may be trademarks or registered trademarks, and are used only for identification and explanation without intent to infringe.

British Library Cataloguing in Publication Data
A catalogue record for this book is available from the British Library

ISBN: 978-1-138-69377-7 (Set)
ISBN: 978-1-315-52921-9 (Set) (ebk)
ISBN: 978-1-138-68344-0 (Volume 17) (hbk)
ISBN: 978-1-138-68345-7 (Volume 17) (pbk)
ISBN: 978-1-315-54448-9 (Volume 17) (ebk)

Publisher's Note
The publisher has gone to great lengths to ensure the quality of this reprint but points out that some imperfections in the original copies may be apparent.

Disclaimer
The publisher has made every effort to trace copyright holders and would welcome correspondence from those they have been unable to trace.

HISTORICAL CRITICISM AND THE MEANING OF TEXTS

J. R. de J. JACKSON

ROUTLEDGE
LONDON AND NEW YORK

First published 1989
by Routledge
11 New Fetter Lane, London EC4P 4EE
29 West 35th Street, New York, NY 10001
© 1989 J. R. de J. Jackson

All rights reserved. No part of this book may be reprinted or reproduced or utilized in any form or by any electronic, mechanical, or other means, now known or hereafter invented, including photocopying and recording, or in any information storage or retrieval system, without permission in writing from the publishers.

British Library Cataloguing in Publication Data
Jackson, J. R. de J. (James Robert de Jager)
Historical criticism and the meaning of texts
1. Literature. Historical criticism
I. Title
801'.95

Library of Congress Cataloging in Publication Data
Jackson, J. R. de J. (James Robert de Jager)
Historical criticism and the meaning of texts.
Bibliography: p.
Includes index.
1. Historical criticism (Literature)   2. Criticism, Textual.   3. Literature – History and criticism – Theory, etc.   4. Literature and history.   5. Literature and society.   I. Title.
PN98.H57J33   1989   801'.95   88–26399
ISBN 0 415 00767 4

FOR HEATHER

CONTENTS

Acknowledgements ix
Introduction 1
1 TRIANGLES OF INTERPRETATION 9
2 DISPLACED ENVIRONMENTS 37
3 KNOWLEDGES OF THE PAST 63
4 STRATEGIES 92
5 THE RELATIONSHIP OF HISTORICAL CRITICISM TO SOME ALTERNATIVE MODES 117
Notes 152
References 168
Index 169

ACKNOWLEDGEMENTS

The preparation of this book was made possible by grants from the Killam Program of the Canada Council and from the Connaught Foundation of the University of Toronto. I am grateful for the encouragement of Michael G. Cooke, George Dekker, David V. Erdman, Jack Stillinger, and Carl Woodring, who kindly agreed to act as referees on my behalf.

Informal conversation with friends who have taken a sympathetic interest in my topic has often alerted me to aspects of it that I had not thought of on my own, and I should like to acknowledge particularly the help of this sort that I have received from J. F. Bosher, W. H. Halewood, and C. Anderson Silber, while adding that none of them was shown the use to which I had put it. My first draft was read by H. J. Jackson and substantial revisions were made in the light of her detailed and constructive criticism.

INTRODUCTION

The term 'historical criticism' has been used rather casually to refer to a number of activities that differ from one another in purpose and scale. Some of them are vaguely conceived or defined and some are narrow and particular. What they have in common is an interest in the recovery of the past.

Interest in the recovery of the past is more properly the field of the historian than of the literary critic, and it is perhaps appropriate that Taine, one of the first to offer an explicit statement of the aims of historical criticism, should have perceived literature as the handmaiden of history, and should have felt satisfied to define the goal of the historical critic as being to 'recover from the monuments of literature a knowledge of the way in which people thought and felt several centuries ago' (p. v). Taine's faith in the value of literature as a historical document has come to seem somewhat naïve to historians a century or more later, as has his Viconian confidence that patterns of development can be discerned by means of it. To literary critics it is his reduction of literature to a historical instrument, his assumption that the past is more important than the work of literature, that seems to be at fault. Whatever its theoretical shortcomings, however, Taine's kind of practical exploration of the ways in which we can improve our awareness of the nature of the past has been absorbed with profit and is now taken for granted by historians and literary critics alike.

However, when one turns to 'historical criticism' thought of as criticism in which literature itself is the *raison d'être*, the term is variously understood. There is, for example, the influential employment of the term by Northrop Frye in his *Anatomy of Criticism*, where he uses it to mean criticism in which an attempt is made to approach the literature of an earlier period without subjecting it to the values of the present. The historical critic, he suggests, 'develops . . . toward total and indiscriminate acceptance: there is nothing "in his field" that he is not prepared to read with interest' (p. 24). Here the emphasis is on the historical critic's deliberate suspension of his own modern point of view and his modern values. This self-denying aspect of historical criticism is seen in a more positive spirit by D. W. Robertson, Jr, in his appeal for 'that kind of literary analysis which seeks to reconstruct the intellectual attitudes and the cultural ideals of a period in order to reach a fuller understanding of its literature' (p. 3). What Robertson had in mind was not merely the suspension of the modern point of view but the definition of the distinctive point of view of a historical period and a temporary adoption of it.

The relationship of the literature of the past to the time in which it was written has traditionally been of interest to literary critics. Generations of them have taken it for granted that one's understanding of literary works is likely to be impaired or even transformed if one is ignorant of the social context in which they were written. This assumption was challenged indirectly by the rise of New Criticism, with its emphasis on close analysis of texts and its impatience with attention to ancillary evidence that it felt was distracting and largely irrelevant. The relations between the historical approach and New Criticism were amicably explored in a pair of papers delivered in 1950 by Cleanth Brooks and A. S. P. Woodhouse. Woodhouse opened the discussion, acknowledging 'the common indictment of the Historical Critic, that he allows a consideration of sources and analogues, and of historical influences generally, to distract his attention from the text'. Brooks in turn conceded that historical criticism and what he called, simply, 'criticism' 'are both necessary and necessary to each other'.[1] The sense that historical criticism and New Criticism divided the field of criticism between them and were distinct if allied seems to have been generally accepted until about twenty years ago. During the past twenty years, however, the dominance of New Criticism has been successfully challenged by a number of vigorously expounded critical approaches and either reintroduced in drastically revised forms, such as deconstruction, or abandoned altogether. And the idea seems to have got about that historical criticism – the uneasy contemporary of New Criticism – is similarly outmoded.

In the recent flurries of critical statement and counter-statement, historical criticism has been notable for its absence. Whether this is because, as Woodhouse remarked, 'historical students of literature have tended to work by a silent instinct of accumulation like the bee' (p. 1,033), or because historical critics by temperament and mental habit find the abstractness of critical theory uncongenial, it is difficult to be sure. The effect of their silence, however, has been to make historical criticism, like the New Criticism with which it used to be paired, appear to be something of an intellectual backwater. The assumption seems to have been that historical criticism, like New Criticism, is merely one of a number of optional critical procedures that may have their day and then sink unlamented into oblivion. But historical criticism, as this essay will try to show, is the necessary and unavoidable counterpart of all critical procedures, and, while it too is subject to change and capable of progress and improvement, the supposition that it can be dispensed with is a delusion. The consequences of its temporary fall from favour are doubly unfortunate: much contemporary criticism deliberately ignores its recent findings, supposing that it can remain independent of them without fundamental loss; and historical criticism itself has been spared the rigorous theoretical examination that has been one of the most valuable contributions of recent critical theory, and is not addressing itself to basic weaknesses in its own methods and assumptions.

Given the variety of the meanings that have been associated with 'historical criticism', it will be obvious that any attempt to examine its claims must begin with a definition that limits it. It seems sensible too to define historical criticism in terms of its aim rather than in terms of its method, on the grounds that the aim should define the method rather than the method the aim, and that, while methods are likely to change as our knowledge and skill change, the aim should remain more or less the same.[2] For the purposes of this essay, therefore, and without any wish to prejudice the use of the term elsewhere, the following definition is proposed: historical criticism is criticism that tries to read past works of literature in the way in which they were read when they were new.

Reading past works of literature in the way in which they were read when they were new is what most naïve readers suppose they are doing already. Experience makes one increasingly aware of the discrepancies between the original readings and subsequent ones, and many sophisticated readers think the discrepancies so great as to be beyond remedy. In proposing such an aim for historical criticism, therefore, some further explanation is required. The formulation has to be qualified in several ways. It is not assumed, for example, that the value of a past work of literature to its readers when it was new has a direct bearing on its value for the historical critic; the historical critic, as historical critic, is concerned only with meaning. It is possible that evidence of originally acknowledged value may help the historical critic to arrive at an understanding of originally perceived meaning, but there its usefulness to historical criticism stops.

It may also be observed that readers are often slow to understand the meaning of new literary works and that the understanding of the readers of past works of literature when they were new is likely to be an unsatisfactory criterion to aim at. A double confusion is involved here. The first is the fundamental one of not distinguishing 'meaning' from 'significance'.[3] What we are proposing is meaning in the sense of the meaning the work conveyed and not in the sense of the meaning (significance) that meaning had for any particular reader at first or later. The second is a confusion that is characteristic of the aesthetics of modernism, to be found in, say, the poetry of T. S. Eliot and Ezra Pound and the novels of Joyce, all of which bewildered many of their original readers. It is tempting to claim that these works are an exception, but in fact the difficulty that their original readers felt on reading them when they were new is part of the experience that the historical critic will wish to preserve or at least to be aware of. To read the *Four Quartets* or *Ulysses* after they have been tamed by half a century of critical commentary and literary imitation is to have an experience that is profoundly different from that of their first readers. We may prefer the tamed version, but historical critics will wish to be able to compare it to the challenge the works first represented.

Finally there is the problem posed by authors who failed to come to grips with their public, because they were eccentric, or socially isolated, or because they did not publish their work. The poetry of Henry Vaughan, of Blake, or the later poetry of Clare, all seem ill suited to the criterion of being understood as they were understood when they were new. But the incongruity is one of the letter and not of the spirit. If there were no readers for a work when it was new then the historical critic will wish to achieve a sense of how the readers who were contemporary with it would have been likely to understand it if they had had the chance. Historical criticism in such circumstances may be unsatisfactorily speculative and its results will be treated with appropriate caution, but it will nevertheless continue to be an essential element in critical activity.

A corollary to the aim of reading past works of literature as they were read when they were new is that historical criticism is not an end in itself but a means to other ends. It is certainly possible for a historical critic to be a historical critic and no more; like scholarly editing, the activity can be intellectually and even aesthetically satisfying in itself. But establishing the original meaning of a text, like establishing the original wording of a text, is normally undertaken with a view to providing reliable materials for all other kinds of criticism to work with.[4] In fact most historical critics are not historical critics only and make a practice of applying other kinds of criticism to the materials they themselves have provided. It may be added that it is virtually impossible for any kind of literary critic to function without indulging in some historical criticism, and that the less conscious and systematic the indulgence is the less bearing the results are likely to have on the work of literature being discussed.

The division of literary criticism into two branches that Woodhouse and Brooks acknowledged in the 1950s was a division into complementary critical responsibilities, not a division into independent and unrelated activities. Historical critics learned from the analytical advances of the New Critics, and, while the New Critics for the most part turned from the active pursuit of historical criticism and urged others to do likewise, they did so from a vantage-point of historical knowledge that they shared with the historical critics who were their contemporaries. From a historical point of view they may be said to have lived off their capital without ever quite exhausting it. But, while their heirs, the formalist critics of the past twenty years, have inherited many of their characteristic strengths, the historical awareness they took for granted is not one of them. In recent years the anachronistic results of determinedly ahistorical formalist criticism have begun to be challenged by historical critics, and efforts have been made to explain the importance of historical criticism by both precept and example.[5]

Hitherto it has proved very difficult to find common ground. One does not regret lacking historical awareness if one has never experienced it consciously. Formalists may agree that historical critics are more likely than themselves to know what a past work of literature meant when it was new without feeling that they are missing very much. Nevertheless a concern for meaning is shared by formalists and historical critics alike, and it seems possible that a re-examination of the elements of literary semantics in terms that are calculated to take into account the effect of the passage of time on meaning will provide a useful bridge between the two.

The book that follows attempts to construct such a bridge. It is made up of five chapters, each of which constitutes a necessary part of a cumulative argument. The overall theme is the nature of historical criticism and an account of the part it plays in all criticism of past literature. The first chapter, 'Triangles of interpretation', reconsiders the traditional analogy between author and work and speaker and utterance in attempts to determine meaning. The limits to a speaker's right to determine meaning are compared to the limits of an author's right, and the roles of hearers and readers relative to one another are assessed. The link between utterances and the environment in which they occur is compared with the link between works of literature and the environments in which they are read. The second chapter, 'Displaced environments', develops the consequences to the environments of works of literature when time passes and their readers take for granted different environments. One of the most important consequences is that if meaning depends on environment (as I argue it must) a change in environment is likely to bring about a change in meaning. A reader or critic may or may not be aware of such change. The third chapter, 'Knowledges of the past', takes up the possibility that such change, while regrettable, is unavoidable. Making use of current theories about the nature of historical knowledge and about the nature of our knowledge of our own personal experience, I concede certain limitations to our recovery of past environments but maintain that the past environments to which literary works refer are more limited and more accessible than the past environments that historians attempt to recover. Chapter 4, 'Strategies', presents a group of methods by which historical criticism may be made more effective than it has been hitherto. This chapter is necessarily speculative but it is also practical. It considers the potential resources of information, showing how they differ from the resources relied upon hitherto; it suggests the stages necessary to the adequate exploitation of these resources and estimates the kind of scholarly co-operation that they will require. The final chapter, 'The relationship of historical criticism to some alternative modes', examines the ways in which some of the currently prevailing modes of criticism help or hinder the practice of historical criticism. Traditional literary history and Frye's archetypal classifications are considered, as are single-genre and single-author specialism; the accidental usefulness of modern evaluative criticism is pointed out, the work of F. R. Leavis and of Marxists and feminists being used as examples; the possibilities of some aspects of structuralism, reader-response theory, and deconstruction for the historical critic are explored.

Historical criticism as it is expounded in this book does not yet exist. Historical criticism as it has been practised hitherto is found wanting, but a case is made, on the ground that historical criticism is both an unavoidable and a necessary part of literary interpretation, for reviving it in a more satisfactory form.

1
TRIANGLES OF INTERPRETATION

For linguistic science it is fundamental that language is an affair not merely of *expression* but also of *impression*, that communication is of its essence, and that in its definition this must not be overlooked.

C. K. Ogden and I. A. Richards

it is in relation to its culture that language has its initial and minimal symbolizing power.

Roy Harvey Pearce

Meaning is more than a matter of intention, it is also a matter of convention.

John R. Searle

I

Literary interpretation traditionally begins at the point at which the meaning of a text is not self-evident.[1] In order to improve imperfect understanding of its meaning it is necessary for the interpreter either to supplement the text by adding to it information that readers previously lacked or to look at the text from a different point of view.[2] Most practical criticism is a mixture of these alternatives, and the roles they play in any particular critic's practice are often difficult to disentangle, but in order to consider their respective claims it has proved convenient in the past to treat them separately and to regard them as being potentially antithetical.

The dichotomy was narrowly defined some years ago by a critic who wished to reject the supposition that interpretations were neither true nor false but a matter of individual preference. In *Validity in Interpretation*, E. D. Hirsch, Jr, attributed current resistance to the belief that literary texts have fixed meanings to the development of the theory that the meaning of texts must be derived from the texts alone – the theory of 'semantic autonomy'. He argued that the theory of semantic autonomy in turn was a consequence of the widespread acceptance of the assumption that authors' intentions before they begin to write or while they are writing are irrelevant to the meaning of the text once it has been written – the theory of 'intentional fallacy'.[3] Hirsch advocated a return to the view that texts mean what their authors meant when they wrote them, and, while he allowed for various exceptions and acknowledged the difficulties involved in establishing what an author meant, he was uncompromising in his assertion that fixed meaning must be either determined by author's meaning or abandoned. As he put it:

> It might be the case that there does not really exist a viable normative ideal that governs the interpretation of texts. This would follow if any of the various arguments brought against the author were to hold. For if the meaning of the text is not the author's, then no interpretation can possibly correspond to the meaning of the text, since the text can have no determinate or determinable meaning.[4]

One can sympathize with Hirsch's aims here without feeling satisfied with his conclusion; in the world of ideas it is difficult to turn the clock back. The problem of finding a criterion of meaning for literary texts is analogous to a related problem in the field of ethics. The ethical problem is that, once one suggests that God's intentions are not an adequate criterion of the way in which people should behave, it seems that there may be no adequate criterion for moral behaviour. Those who believe in God have often emphasized this dangerous moral consequence of scepticism.[5] The lack of a fixed moral criterion impinges more directly and urgently on our lives than the lack of a fixed literary criterion does, and we are less able to contemplate it in a spirit of disinterested investigation; we look immediately for other criteria – the common good, social convention, and so on. God's 'intentions' come to be regarded as a traditional summing up or shorthand for the accumulated wisdom of civilization. 'Commandments' come to be considered as an end rather than as a beginning – rules of behaviour that human beings have devised and that human beings may criticize and challenge, but that have too much weight of social verification behind them to be dismissed along with their mythical inventor. We resist the dictum 'God's criterion or none' because it is intolerable. Hirsch's insistence on the formula 'author's criterion or none' is unsatisfactory in a similar way, and his clear statement may well have had the unintended effect of confirming the proponents of semantic autonomy in the assumption that there was no rational alternative to it.[6]

While critical theory has identified the question of deciding what a literary work means as a crucial one, it has not resolved it; critics have agreed to differ. Indecision on this issue may be allowable for practical critics in general, but it is not a satisfactory state of mind for historical critics. The attempt to read past works of literature as they were read when they were new assumes that when they were new they were read in one way rather than another (or in some ways rather than in others). The efforts of historical criticism have been directed to finding out what that way was. The possibility of determining a fixed meaning seems, therefore, to be a presupposition of historical criticism, and proponents of historical criticism have an obligation to explain or at least know why they believe in it.

The practice of reading past works of literature as they were read when they were new is arrived at by analogy with the practice of reading new works of literature. In considering the way in which the historical critic arrives at the meaning of a past work of literature, it seems appropriate therefore to begin by examining yet again the general question of the way in which readers arrive at the meaning of new literary works and only then to consider what differences, if any, are to be found in the procedure of the historical critic.

Like most of the complicated activities that we indulge in habitually, reading resists definition, the experience seeming to vary so greatly from reader to reader, from work to work, and even from occasion to occasion that the would-be theorist is left grappling with a Proteus.[7] But one of the few aspects of reading on which there seems to be general agreement is the semantic model of the elements involved in arriving at the meaning of a literary text. The three elements are the text itself, the author (without whom there would be no text), and the reader (without whom the question of the meaning of the text would not arise). The existence of the three elements is undeniable, and as long as the meaning of the text is arrived at without difficulty all is well. It is when the meaning arrived at by one reader is incompatible with the meaning arrived at by another reader that arguments arise about the propriety of appealing for help to the author. Hirsch's claim for the authority of the author takes for granted not only the truth of the three-element model of meaning but also its adequacy. It does not consider the possibility that while for uncomplicated cases the three-element model will suffice, it is only a model, a convenient over-simplification, and that other elements may also play a part even in the straightforward reading of a text.

Semantics was not developed in order to serve critical theory. Literary criticism usually remains at a respectful distance from it, borrowing its conclusions without necessarily rehearsing the steps that led to them, and it is dependent to a greater extent than it usually realizes on semantic assumptions that it may or may not share. In the past the problem of meaning has been approached from two different points of view and has relied on two different kinds of evidence. The two different points of view are the philosophical and the philological or linguistic;[8] the two different kinds of evidence are derived from the analysis of thought (the emphasis being on what we think or feel) and examination of language (the emphasis being on how language expresses what we think or feel). On the whole philosophers have tended to be more aware of the first kind of evidence and philologists of the second kind, and it will be apparent that from the point of view of the student of meaning (who may be neither a philosopher nor a philologist) the emphasis of the first kind of evidence is on the producer (speaker, thinker, writer) and the emphasis of the second kind is on the consumer (hearer, reader). These emphases are harmless enough as long as an argument does not arise on some such unanticipated issue as the disputed meaning of a literary text for which neither the philosophical nor the philological approach was meant to be employed. But, when the critical dispute is joined by parties who, though neither philosophical nor philological, differ from one another in taking for granted a philosophical or philological bias respectively, mutual misunderstanding is almost unavoidable.

In the twentieth century just such a misunderstanding seems to have come about. There appears to be a fundamental difference between the semantic models presupposed by literary critics in the English-speaking world and literary critics in the French-speaking world.[9] When the two worlds meet at the level of literary criticism, as they have been doing during the past twenty years, there is mutual incomprehension and consequent distrust because the semantic foundations of their critical assumptions are not made explicit. The development of thought in the western world is not usually so parochial; in this case the existence of two mutually uncomprehending and mutually unaware intellectual traditions is the result of historical accident and of the artificial boundaries between different academic disciplines.

In the seventeenth century both the English-speaking and the French-speaking worlds were active contributors to the development of a theory of knowledge, the philosophical point of view. Language was considered in this context because it was evidence of 'internal conceptions' and the means by which 'the thoughts of men's minds [might] be conveyed from one to another'.[10] Locke's pre-eminence in English philosophy influenced the role that the study of language played in it and seems to have determined the way in which questions about meaning were asked by empirical philosophers thereafter. This approach reappears in a speaker-centred semantics in which the speaker is portrayed as trying to convey a clear idea to a hearer by means of a more or less adequate expression of it in language. Noam Chomsky has pointed out that 'from this conception of language, it is only a short step to the association of the creative aspect of language use with true artistic creativity',[11] and that there should be a correlation between the semantic model and the expressive theory of creativity that developed side by side with it during the eighteenth and nineteenth centuries is not surprising.[12] The philological counterpart to this thought-centred approach seems to have petered out towards the end of the eighteenth century, leaving the field clear for philosophers, semanticists, and literary critics.

Philology, however, had been undergoing a revolution of its own.[13] A series of thinkers in France, most notably Condillac and Taine, made it possible to replace the concept of language as the invention and means of expression for thought with a concept of language as an elaborate system of signs that deserves to be examined on its own account and that may be what has made thought itself possible. This way of approaching the subject is developed most influentially in Saussure's *Course in General Linguistics*, and its effect is to emphasize the arbitrary nature of the relationship between language and things, and the extent to which our sense of things is defined by the words we use to denote them; it regards the utterances of individual speakers as selections and combinations of a linguistic system that is inherited.[14] Its emphasis is on convention, on relationship, and on the communication of materials that are already familiar to both the speaker and the hearer. The confrontation of these priorities with the expectations of the English-speaking empirical school is amusingly exhibited in Ogden and Richards's semantic classic *The Meaning of*

Meaning, where a paragraph begins: 'How great is the tyranny of language over those who propose to inquire into its workings is well shown in the speculations of the late F. de Saussure. . . . he obeys blindly the primitive impulse to infer from a word some object for which it stands, and sets out determined to find it' (p. 4).

Sixty-five years later the theories of Saussure are not so casually dismissed, but the semantic conflict rarely surfaces in so undisguised a form. When problems of literary meaning arise, critics fall back on traditional semantic assumptions, usually without being conscious that alternative traditions exist. A subsequent bias towards faith in the author or faith in the text is likely to be determined by the tradition to which they happen to appeal. But neither tradition ever aspired to provide an adequate basis for settling disputes about literary meaning, and while both are elaborate and absorbing their energy is expended on problems that are at most analogous to the problems of literary interpretation. Without trying to replace or rival either the philosophical or the philological tradition, it seems possible to provide a modified if elementary model for the process of arriving at literary meaning that may be tested against any reader's experience and that avoids the dichotomy confronted by Hirsch by anticipating it at the semantic level. To do this it is necessary to begin, as semanticists have commonly done, with the experience of spoken language, deriving a formula from the examination of simple and familiar examples that can be agreed upon readily, before proceeding to apply the formula to the more complex instances that require clarification.

II

In our communications with one another, the question 'What do you mean?' is the exception rather than the rule. Most of the time when we speak we are understood and when we listen to others speaking we understand what they say. Understanding is not a wholly self-conscious activity; like walking, it is the almost automatic performance of a skill we cannot remember having lacked.

Two important exceptions to these statements must be admitted at the outset, both of them having to do with the experience of learning. The first exception is the experience of children, who by comparison with adults are imperfectly familiar with their native language and with the objects that constitute their world; their predicament resembles the phase of learning to walk that they have already passed through. The second exception is the experience of adults who are being instructed in the terminology and concepts of an unfamiliar subject; they may be likened to experienced walkers who are attempting to master dancing. Apart from these two exceptions, the question 'What do you mean?' is usually a sign of failure on the part of the speaker or the hearer, or of both; it signals an interruption in the process of communication. The way in which such failures occur can most readily be understood if the way in which successful communications take place is considered first.

Our communications with one another depend upon a shared language and a shared environment. By 'language' is meant here not only speech and writing but also gestures and facial expressions; by 'environment' is meant both our physical surroundings including our bodies, our social practices and organizations, and our mental circumstances, including our knowledge and feelings. The original relationship of environment to language is a speculative matter, but at present environment seems to be the dominant factor, being influenced in its turn and even changed in certain ways by language.[15]

The importance of sharing a language is evident to anyone who has travelled to a foreign-language area that is off the tourist track without first learning even the rudiments of the language. Like Gulliver with the Lilliputians, one is forced to rely on mime to acquire the necessities of life and is likely to be regarded in consequence as mentally defective. Moreover, even if a language is shared, regional differences in it can lead to failures of communication.

The importance of sharing an environment is perhaps less obvious, since for practical purposes the environments of the industrialized world closely resemble one another, but again Gulliver's difficulties in explaining the uses of gunpowder to the King of Brobdingnag who was ignorant of the substance and his equally troublesome explanation of the nature of lying to his Houyhnhnm master which ends lamely in the circumlocution 'saying the thing which is not' are representative examples.

The individual inherits an environment and a language that are already complete and seems to learn how to communicate with others by imitating the communications of others with him or her. Once skill in communication is sufficient to satisfy the needs of the individual, the process of learning usually ceases, and a resistance to subsequent changes in language and changes in environment is often to be observed.[16] During the process of learning, deviations from prevalent usage and untypical perceptions of environment are penalized by failure of communication. The child who calls a chair a table or who uses a table as a chair is summarily corrected.

Among adults most communication takes place with reference to a shared environment and by means of a shared language. When an unfamiliar aspect of the environment is mentioned or unfamiliar words or turns of phrase are used we are immediately at a loss and may be obliged to ask for an explanation or to apply our minds to what the speaker probably meant. Such occasions for asking 'What do you mean?' are relatively rare and may be classed with the second exception mentioned above – adults undergoing instruction. The assumption of the question is that the speaker is one of a group of people whose experience differs from the questioner's own.

In ordinary discourse we understand the meaning of what is said by using what may be thought of as a triangle of interpretation. The triangle of linguistic interpretation is a mirror image of what may be thought of as a triangle of linguistic utterance.[17] Each of these triangles requires the juxtaposition of three elements, and the absence of any one of them makes communication impossible. The most obvious element is the utterance itself; the other two elements are the language in which the utterance is made and the situation in which it is made.[18] The three elements are employed together by the speaker (utterer) in order to say something that a hearer can understand; they are employed together by the hearer in order to understand what has been said. The triangles may be said to be mirror images of one another because although they consist of the same elements the elements are employed by each in the opposite sequence. A speaker comments on an environment or refers to it by seeking and finding a suitable utterance in language; a hearer interprets an utterance by seeking and finding a meaning in language and then applying it to the situation.

The triangle of linguistic utterance may be represented diagrammatically as in figure 1. An example of this process would be the utterance 'I am hungry'. The speaker begins by being aware of his need for food (the situation); he then searches for the conventional words for communicating that need in language; and having found them he utters them. The conscious part of the speaker's mental activity (unless he is being obliged to communicate in a foreign language) is likely to be limited to his sense of the situation; if

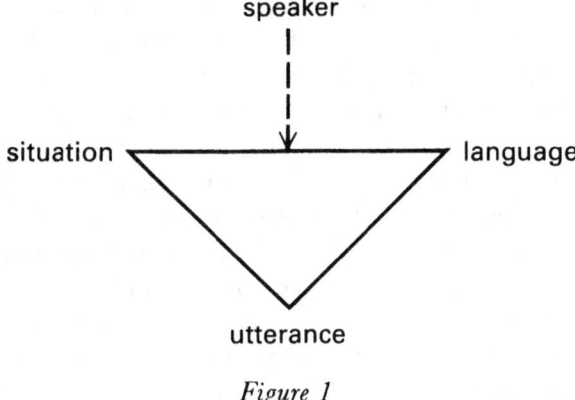

Figure 1

the situation is familiar the words for it may come through force of habit by a process of association.

The triangle of linguistic interpretation, conversely, may be represented diagrammatically as in figure 2. To continue with the same example, if the utterance is 'I am hungry', the hearer will match it with conventional language to find its usual range of meaning and will then compare that with the speaker's apparent situation. Only then will the meaning of the utterance be interpreted. At that point the hearer may respond by giving the speaker food.

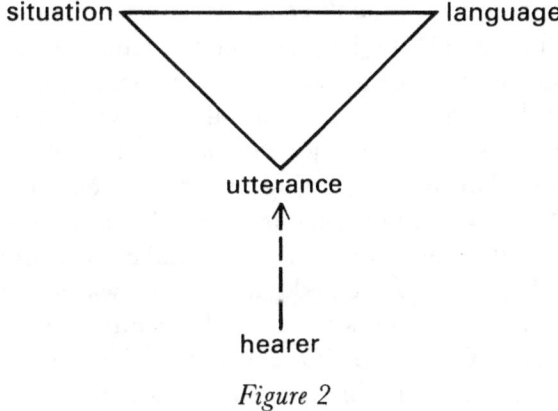

Figure 2

An untypically simple utterance has been offered as an example in order to make the working of the triangles of utterance and interpretation clear; by complicating it a little the need for a process of interpretation becomes more obvious. If a speaker says 'I am hungry' and the hearer compares the utterance with language, identifying its usual range of meanings, and then compares those with the fact that the speaker has been eating for three hours and has just pushed his chair back from a table where his half-empty plate is clearly visible (situation), the hearer will perceive a contradiction between the language and the situation. In order to interpret the meaning of the statement it is necessary to juxtapose language and situation. If the speaker is smiling, or if his eyes twinkle, or if we know him to be fond of irony, we may consider the possibility that he is being ironical, that he means, in fact, the opposite of what he has said. The hearer would interpret 'I am hungry' as meaning 'I am satisfied'. But if the speaker is not known as a humorist and looks serious and raises an empty glass, and the hearer observes that there is nothing on the table to drink, the possibility will arise that the language is at fault. The speaker may be a foreigner who meant to say 'I am thirsty' but chose the wrong linguistic formula. In such a case the hearer might ask whether he meant 'I am thirsty' and supply his need if the answer was affirmative. A third possibility is that the speaker has gone mad, a fact to be ascertained by further observation of the situation. In each case the triangle of interpretation is applied in order to arrive at meaning.[19]

As long as an utterance is phrased in language that is familiar to us and refers to a situation that we know by experience, understanding will be immediate and we shall be unconscious of the mental process involved. When either the language or the situation is outside our experience or contrary to it, however, the effort made to solve the resulting puzzle suggests that the normal unconscious mental process involves comparison and that a discrepancy alerts our mind to the need to think. The act of putting on shoes seems to be roughly analogous. We put them on unconsciously, by habit, generally with our mind on other things; but if by mistake we begin to put on someone else's shoes we are suddenly made aware not only of the discrepancy but also of the way in which we must normally react to the familiar feel of our own shoes. It seems that when we hear an utterance our minds combine the words (language) and the thing (situation), so long as they are already familiar to the mind, to arrive at a meaning.

This obscure process seems to work well even if the combination is new, but not if either the words or the things to which they refer are. Often in such situations the mind has the resources to solve the puzzle. If someone uses the word 'hylozoism', for instance, a knowledge of elementary Greek will suggest that two Greek words, *hyle* (matter) and *zoe* (life), are being combined to mean the belief that life is material or that material is alive, and the context of the words may confirm this guess. Alternatively, if someone mentions an electric toothbrush, even if we have never heard of one before and may think of the idea as ridiculous, we may be able to understand what is meant by it and to visualize it after a fashion, and if we encounter one later we shall probably recognize what it is.

If we cannot solve the puzzle for ourselves, we may well ask, 'What does "hylozoism" mean?' or 'What is an electric toothbrush?' or 'What do you mean by "hylozoism" or by "an electric toothbrush"?' In such questions the emphasis is not on the special meaning of the speaker (the *you*) but on the conventional meaning of the word or the conventional nature of the thing. We are acknowledging a deficiency in our own knowledge and seeking to remedy it so that we may understand what is being said just as people better informed than ourselves might be expected to understand it. The discrepancy that we have noticed is one that existed in ourselves; our environment or our language differed from the norms of a group of other people.

A failure of communication can also arise from the speaker's deficiency. If, for example, the speaker used the word 'hylozoism' to mean 'dualism' (the belief that the soul and the body are separate entities) in some such sentence as 'We need not accept the hylozoism of Descartes', we might, if we were acquainted with the conventional view of Descartes's beliefs, ask, 'What do you mean?' The point of the question would be to find out whether an unusual sense was being given to the word or whether an unusual view of Descartes was being offered. The same process of comparison of utterance with situation (Descartes) and language (hylozoism) would be taking place, but if both the situation and the language were familiar it would be the combination of these elements rather than the elements themselves that were unfamiliar; the discrepancy would be between the unfamiliar combination offered (Descartes–hylozoism) and the familiar combination expected (Descartes–dualism). Subsequent explanation might show that the speaker had confused the two terms and would result in an amended statement. If subsequent explanation revealed either that the conventional notion of Descartes's thought needed to be amended or that the conventional notion of the meaning of 'hylozoism' was wrong, we should merely have an example of the kind of misunderstanding previously described as a deficiency of the hearer (in turn a repetition of the learning situation). But we should be inclined to dismiss the mere assertion of the speaker that Descartes's views were not what they are generally supposed to be or that 'hylozoism' did not mean what it is generally supposed to mean unless we had further reasons to believe the speaker to be especially knowledgeable about such matters; and even if we had such further reasons we should probably remain sceptical.

In only three sorts of case does the question 'What do you mean?' constitute a genuine request that a speaker determine the meaning of his or her statement without reference to other authority. The first and most common case arises when a statement is ambiguous. A statement can be ambiguous either because its reference to the environment is ambiguous or because its use of language is ambiguous.[20] If we ask someone in a city how to find our way to a particular shop and are told, 'Take the third turning to the right', we might ask, 'Do you mean the third turning counting the street beside us or the third turning after it?' We shall accept the speaker's determination of what was meant as a clarification ('Oh, I mean the third turning after it' or 'Oh, I was counting this street as the first'). But the speaker's determination will be accepted only if it confirms one of the options we have anticipated. If the speaker says, 'Actually I meant the third turning to the left' or 'I meant either', we shall probably seek advice from someone else. The speaker's authority over ambiguous statement is limited to choice of one of two (or more) options in which situation and language are conventionally used.

The second case is that of a statement that is inadequately determined and open to conflicting interpretations. For example, A may ask B and C to paint his house and they may agree to a price for doing so. Before the painting begins B and C may disagree about whether painting the house includes stripping off the old paint first. B may say, 'I assumed that we would be doing that', to which C may respond, 'But if I had thought we were going to do that I would never have agreed to such a low price.' If they attempt to determine the meaning of their agreement by asking A what he had in mind, he may resolve the issue by confirming B's view (in which case the agreement will probably have to be renegotiated) or by confirming C's. But if, as is possible, he had not thought about the advantage of stripping the old paint off before the new paint was applied he might be tempted to maintain that he had meant that in the first place. His contention would be difficult to dispute (it is difficult to tell what is in a speaker's mind apart from what he or she says), but that the work for which a certain price was quoted could be defined by him later in this way would almost certainly be disputed. If the matter were taken before a court of law the issue would not be what the speaker meant, but what his statement would have meant when made by most people in the community. What the speaker meant may matter to him or to those who care about his feelings (as the conscientious B may have done), but it is not usually allowed to determine the meaning of the statement he made.

The third case is that of a statement that does not seem to make sense. If it is made by someone in his right mind and sober and appears not to be a joke we may ask, 'What do you mean?' An example might be the statement 'The sun did shine so cold'. The language involved in the statement is familiar but the environment referred to seems to be impossibly at odds with the environment we know. The speaker might respond that his statement was a comment on a previous statement of ours that had seemed foolishly improbable and that he had quoted the improbable statement of Wordsworth's Idiot Boy as a suitable parallel. In such a case the original statement might be compared to an enthymeme (a syllogism missing one of its steps) that could be understood only if one possessed some bit of unstated information. Again the appeal for an explanation is apparently to the speaker but the answer is confined to supplying the deficiency in terms already familiar to a group of people.

III

An analogy between 'speech acts' and works of literature is often taken for granted by critics interested in criteria of meaning.[21] Speech acts have the advantage of being familiar to all of us, both in our capacity as speakers and in our capacity as hearers. They have the further advantage of being relatively simple, even if inconveniently various. The analogy is useful but imperfect, and unless we are aware of its limitations it is liable to lead us astray.

The most obvious discrepancy between a statement and a work of literature is one of scale and hence of complexity. A spoken statement may be compared with a statement in a work of literature. When Hamlet says, 'There are more things in heaven and earth than are dreamt of in your philosophy', we can understand the literal meaning of his remark very much as if it were made to us by someone we know. When he says, 'I know a hawk from a handsaw', we do not wholly understand him because we are not sure why anyone would be expected to confuse a hawk with a handsaw. We may wonder whether by 'hawk' and 'handsaw' he means what people usually mean nowadays, but we guess from its context that the general meaning of his statement is that he knows what's what, he is not to be easily fooled. The process here seems to be almost identical to our interpretation of any statement using terms that are unexpected or not self-explanatory. One could go through an entire play (or novel, or poem) taking each statement in turn and treating it as if it were a speech act. At this level of application the analogy seems to hold.

Difficulties begin to appear, however, if the analogy is applied more sweepingly to embrace the whole work of literature rather than the individual statements of which it is composed. If we take the statement 'I am tired of life', for example, and compare it with *Hamlet*, arguing that the view expressed in *Hamlet* is essentially 'I am tired of life', a much bolder analogy is involved. The meaning of one relatively unambiguous statement is being compared with a conclusion about the cumulative effect of a very large number of statements, some of which are by no means unambiguous. The discrepancy would be less, perhaps, if we were to listen to someone talking for an afternoon and conclude that what his talk signified, even if he did not say these very words, was that he was tired of life. Here we are referring to the meaning of statements in a different sense, indeed in rather the manner used by Freud when he discusses dreams and their meanings. We have moved beyond the words said to speculation about what prompted them. This procedure is followed on the assumption that the speaker is revealing something about himself that is different from the meaning he is trying to convey (as, for example, when someone whose feelings have been hurt cracks a joke but cannot make himself smile at the end of it).

One of the crucial differences between works of literature and conversation is that they are not spontaneous. Another is that, unlike talk in which speakers do not commonly anticipate in their early statements what they may say in their later ones and frequently forget in their later statements what they have said in their earlier ones, a work of literature is usually contemplated as a whole by its author before it is placed before the public and is usually thought of as a whole (although it may undergo change in the process of composition) before it is written. Furthermore the author expects it to be understood as a whole. Seeing *Hamlet*, or reading it, is not like spending three hours hearing Shakespeare talk.

The difference between determining the meaning of an utterance and determining the meaning of a work of literature is twofold. The first part of the difference is that the work of literature consists of many utterances whose meaning is generally cumulative as they are perceived as being related to one another in groups or as a whole. The second part of the difference is that the environments of author and audience are not mutually observable – unlike speakers and hearers, they are not in one another's presence. What may be called 'literary interpretation', as distinct from the 'linguistic interpretation' that we have considered hitherto, is a process that works in a similar way but uses slightly different materials.

The force of the analogy between a speech act and a work of literature is not derived from the similarity between speech acts and works of literature but from a similarity between the way in which we grasp the meaning of a speech act and the way in which we grasp the meaning of a work of literature.[22] The process of understanding a work of literature resembles the process of understanding an utterance in that it too consists of three elements and may be represented diagrammatically as triangular. Two of the three elements involved are different, however. In place of utterance, language, and situation, we have *text*, *language*, and *environment*. Language is the same in both triangles of interpretation, a conventional medium of communication whose conventions precede the utterance (or the text) and which exists independently of the speaker (author) and of the hearer (reader, audience). The text differs in several significant ways from the utterance or speech act. It is written and its author is not present when it is read; it is repeatable in whole or in part; its readership is not restricted to those its author had in mind.

Environment, which replaces situation, is a different element in a more complicated way. Since author and reader are not in one another's presence as speaker and hearer normally are, they do not automatically share a situation; the reader cannot observe the author's situation and neither expects to nor is expected to. Instead the author takes for granted an environment that the putative reader may be expected to share. This environment in turn is contributed to by two sources of experience, one social and one literary. The *social environment* includes potentially all the aspects of life that are shared by both readers and non-readers; the *literary environment* includes potentially all the aspects of life that are experienced through reading. Readers' awareness of their environment is derived both from their experience of living in general and from their experience of reading in particular. An author takes for granted both these experiences in readers; together the experiences provide the counterpart of the hearer's situation in a speech act.

The triangle of literary interpretation may be represented diagrammatically as in figure 3. The process of interpretation that takes place when we read popular literature is the literary counterpart of the process of interpretation that takes place when we listen to ordinary discourse. We are scarcely aware of it because it has become habitual as one of the features of learning to read. In what follows, the functioning of language will be taken for granted, being essentially the same as it was in the triangle of linguistic interpretation.

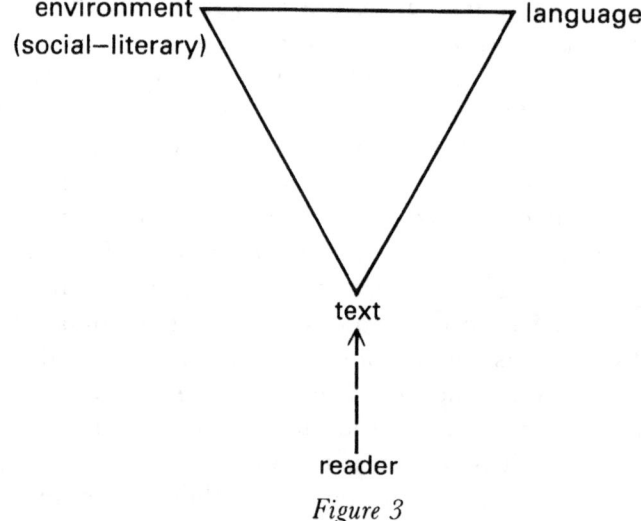

Figure 3

In the triangle of literary interpretation (figure 3), 'text' is the term that corresponds to 'utterance' in the triangle of linguistic interpretation (figure 2). By 'text', however, is meant not just a written utterance – a sentence, for example – but a work of literature. The text may be short (a sonnet or a limerick) or long (an epic or a novel). A text is usually read silently and privately but it may be read aloud to listeners, and in the case of a play it is usually performed before an audience. A text is made up of an accumulation of utterances – in most cases an accumulation of accumulations of utterances – that together constitute a whole.

The form of text most common to the experience of the modern reader is the novel. Most of us are so used to reading novels that we do so without any distinct awareness of our mental processes and without any sense of searching for meaning. We read novels very much as we listen to ordinary conversation, understanding conventional expressions of conventional topics by habit rather than by analysis. This unselfconscious experience is interrupted only when something puzzles us; just as walkers may be startled by tripping on uneven ground into consciousness of the need to place their feet more deliberately, readers who find that they have lost the drift of a novel will pause, reread, and submit the hitherto largely unconscious elements of interpretation to deliberate examination. At this point the triangle of literary interpretation which has hitherto been at work in the residual form of habit becomes active in a conscious way. Just as in the triangle of linguistic interpretation an utterance is juxtaposed with language and situation, so, in the triangle of literary interpretation, the text is juxtaposed with language and environment.

In the triangle of literary interpretation, 'environment' is the term that corresponds to 'situation' in the triangle of linguistic interpretation. In the same way that utterances are understood with reference to the situation to which they refer, texts are understood with reference to the environments to which they refer. However, whereas the situation is observed, the environment is imagined. In a novel, for example, the characters and the action are set in a world that is described or implied. When we read the novel we are stimulated to imagine as much of the described or implied world as is necessary for us to follow the plot, and if the novel is to be effective an author's readers must be in possession of enough of this environment for such imagining to be possible. If what is supplied is inadequate or self-contradictory the reader will have difficulty in understanding the novel. The presentation of environment in a work of literature is highly selective. The nature of the selection differs, of course, from work to work, but there are certain conventions of selection that are usually observed.

The most important convention is that the selection should be limited to those aspects of environment that are shared by the reader. In a sense this requirement is obvious; if the world and the assumptions of a contemporary novel are unrecognizable to the reader, the reader will be unable to understand the novel. The requirement that the environment be a shared one is comparable to the fact that a situation is shared or observable in a speech act. But, while the impracticality of a totally unshared environment is obvious, the meaning of a shared environment is difficult to define. There are, however, several distinguishable elements of environment, such as setting, daily routine, matters of public concern, etc., that may be used as samples for exploration.[23]

Setting, or the physical location of the action of a novel, is perhaps the simplest to deal with. If a novel is set in London, for example, it is common for London streets, districts, and landmarks to be referred to – sometimes for verisimilitude, sometimes for atmosphere, sometimes to further the plot and develop its characters. The ways in which one moves around London (on foot, by bus or underground, by taxi or suburban train), the sorts of occupation associated with the various districts (finance in the City, the law at the Inns of Court, government in Whitehall, theatre on the South Bank, in the West End, and in the Barbican, fashion on the King's Road), the forms of entertainment, manners of dining out, types of dress – all these are familiar even to tourists. And, since many novels are set in London, it is possible for habitual readers to learn much of the familiar detail without ever going there. A London author takes a knowledge of London for granted, but also accepts certain limitations to that knowledge. Piccadilly may be common ground, but if Lamb's Conduit Street is referred to its district is likely to be mentioned or the street itself may be described.

The London environment has been a shared assumption of fiction for so long that it transcends firsthand experience. Indeed, for readers outside the literary capitals, the setting of fiction is almost taken for granted as being a kind of fiction too, or a branch of travel literature. Does the provincial reader miss anything that the London reader will notice? The answer to this question will vary from work to work, but it is easy to conceive of cases in which the environment of a London novel might include details of setting that only a Londoner would appreciate, or that it might include deliberate inaccuracies of setting that only a Londoner would detect. If the details or the inaccuracies are integral to understanding the plot, whole groups of readers are likely to differ in their understanding of the novel. This different understanding will in certain cases be misunderstanding. But, misunderstandings apart, there is a genuine difference of expectation when provincial readers read novels about London. They mentally visualize the streets named less exactly if at all. One of the special pleasures of provincial literature for provincial readers is to read novels in which the environment is their own; the experience reminds them of what they must regularly miss in fiction emanating from the capitals.

Insufficient grasp of the setting of a work is complicated in the case of physical location by the feeling of non-Londoners (to which the preponderance of London literature contributes) that the London environment is a human norm in a way that their own is not. The same might be said of settings in exclusive institutions (universities, public schools, social clubs, etc.) when the readers know of them only by report. When the setting is not sanctioned by social or literary tradition, however, readers are much less likely to be tolerant of unfamiliar details. Their reaction will resemble that of readers in the capital who read works in which the setting is provincial.

Works of literature emanate from so many places nowadays that most readers are used to passing over some unfamiliar details, treating them as dispensable symptoms of realism perhaps. Where the environment is unfamiliar the effect may be compared with seeing an object through a lens that is slightly out of focus. When the action of an American novel takes place on Main Street, it is not necessary to know which town is being referred to; Main Street is understood to be an undifferentiated short form for the main street of small American towns, on the assumption that if you have seen one you have seen them all.

Environment encompasses not only setting but the whole of the world imagined in the novel. It includes our shared knowledge of the conventions of behaviour governing the relations of men and women, of parents and children, of employers and employees; our shared knowledge of currency, transportation, clothing, shops, offices, factories, sport, and so on. Within our own community an enormous amount of such information may be taken for granted. One has only to move to a different community, however, to find that the community of knowledge has changed too. If we read novels written by and for members of another community we become used to coping with occasional difficulties in our perception of the element of environment.

The literary environment shares crucial characteristics with the social environment. Just as each person's experience of life is unique, each person's experience of reading is unique. Nevertheless books presume a substantial shared experience of reading, just as they presume a substantial shared experience of life. The origin of literature, like the origin of language, is obscure; we find it difficult to imagine how the first story could have been told, just as we find it difficult to imagine how the first statement could have been made. Both stories and statements in our experience seem to require precedents in order to be understood. Literature as we know it is written by authors who have read literature and for readers who have read literature. This shared literary environment is as essential to our interpretation of a text as a shared social environment is, but perhaps because we experience it more privately we are less conscious of it.

The effect of the literary environment is most familiar to the generality of readers in forms such as detective fiction and western films. People read detective fiction and watch westerns in the expectation that they will experience variations on a familiar norm. Jaded readers of detective fiction will expect to be provided with a crime, a group of suspects, and a solver of the crime. They will expect to share the solver's investigation and to sympathize with it, but they will not expect to anticipate the solution. The old maxims, 'The butler did it' or 'Cherchez la femme', reflect these expectations, and Agatha Christie managed to score a hit in *The Murder of Roger Ackroyd* in 1926 by breaking with precedent and having the narrator turn out to be the murderer. Similarly, in a western, a town that is in the grip of lawlessness will be tamed by a visitor who, having tamed it, will depart, generally riding on a white horse. In Fred Zinnemann's *High Noon* of 1952 the convention was exploited to considerable effect by changing the visitor into a marshal who has just retired from his job on the day of his marriage to a Quaker. Here the convention that the hero must face the outlaws is brought into conflict with his obligations to his new bride with her Quaker abhorrence of violence. All readers and filmgoers become familiar with such conventions in the same elaborate and subtle but unthinking way in which they become familiar with their social environment, and their appreciation of what they read or see depends upon their acquaintance with the conventions.

The literary environment we share is also made up of our cultural myths. These are acquired partly by reading, partly at second hand by way of education, formal and informal. They are usually part of our consciousness while we are still very young. The materials of these cultural myths are exceedingly diverse, mingling Bible narratives and parables with fairy-tales and stories such as *Robinson Crusoe, Gulliver's Travels,* Sherlock Holmes, the Knights of the Round Table, and Robin Hood.[24] If one happens to miss some part of this tradition – *The Wind in the Willows*, say – the assumption made by the texts we read that it is familiar will gradually give Badger, Ratty, and Toad an existence in our imaginations even if we never repair the oversight. These aspects of the literary environment impinge upon our interpretation of texts as we accept similarities and analogies unthinkingly but are brought up short by discrepancies. Fundamental principles are established, such as the requirement of 'poetic justice', and we are troubled, or at least made attentive, by departures from them.

There is another level of the literary environment that is taken for granted by authors of all but the most popular forms of literature: a corpus of literature that it is assumed a reader will have read. Literary environment in this sense is as various and resistant to definition as our myths are, although the curricula set out by university departments of English often look like attempts to provide such a literary environment ready made. The larger part of this literature was written between about 1585 and 1940; to it may be added a number of exceptionally popular works written during the past forty years. These works are not only alluded to; along with every book each reader has read, they may be said to contribute to forming each reader's expectations of a new text and to be the part of these expectations that an author can count on.

As with the triangle of linguistic interpretation, the triangle of literary interpretation works without our being aware of it until a failure of communication occurs. When such a failure occurs, readers expect to repair it either by altering their awareness of the literary environment or by altering their awareness of the social environment or by altering their awareness of both. If these methods fail, a reader may suspect a lapse on the part of the author.

Take, for instance, a passage such as the following:

Martha walked slowly along the Strand, abstracting her attention from the roar of the traffic, and turned gratefully into the relative stillness of Lincoln's Inn Fields. Her languid progress brought her too soon to the hurly-burly of Queensway and Southampton Row, and when she finally reached Russell Square she felt obliged to sit down on one of the striped deckchairs that decorated the grass in order to compose her thoughts for the dreaded interview.

For many readers, whatever they may think about its literary quality, the passage will seem straightforward. Any reader who is familiar with the part of London being described, however, will recognize that Queensway does not belong there. The passage conflicts with a Londoner's sense of the social environment, and in the absence of any further evidence one might guess that Queensway has been substituted for Kingsway (which would fit), and that the author or even the typesetter has made a mistake. But, if the passage occurs in a novel in which someone from abroad is represented as writing a story with a London setting, the mistake may be deliberately included as a symptom of the newcomer's ignorance. In either case readers who find the social environment of the novel at odds with their own social environment will be awakened to a critical awareness. If the mistake is the author's, the awakening will be a flaw in the reader's experience of the book; if, on the other hand, the mistake was deliberate, the failure on the part of non-London readers may be regarded as a flaw in their experience of the book. For a book to work as it should its social environment and that of its reader must be shared.

A breakdown in the literary environment is just as easy to imagine. Take, for example, the following description of an exchange at a dinner table:

> Sir John was taken by surprise by the Earl's question. He gazed ruminatively at the table and then slowly raised his glass of port to eye level as if assessing its colour. 'I'm afraid this is corked,' he said, 'bring me the other decanter, James.' The butler laughed appreciatively at this remark, but did as he was told.

Many modern readers have never seen a butler and they may have little acquaintance with earls or port, but they will know from their reading that butlers do not laugh appreciatively at their employers' jokes. Here the literary environment has departed from the norm we are used to, not the social environment (although the social environment of an earlier period also lies behind the literary environment of our own time). Again, the reader's critical awareness is awakened. Is this butler really someone else in disguise? Are he and his employer conspiring to poison a guest? Solutions of this kind might explain the passage, which in such cases would have the effect of drawing to our attention the fact that something unusual was going on. Alternatively the passage might merely reflect the author's imperfect acquaintance with literary butlers.

The division of environment into social and literary acknowledges the two different sources of experience that are juxtaposed with the language of a text to produce meaning in the triangle of literary interpretation, but we cannot always distinguish between the sources of our experience in this way, and the divisions between them are often indistinct. Take a passage like the following, for example:

> Mr Salteena awoke next morning in his small but pleasant room. It was done in green and white with monograms on the toilet set. He had a tiny white bed with a green quilt and a picture of the Nativity and one of Windsor Castle on the walls. The sun was shining over all these things as Mr Salteena opened his sleepy eyes. Just then there was a rat tat on the door. 'Come in' called Mr Salteena and in came Edward Procurio balancing a tray very cleverly. He looked most elegant with his shiny black hair and pale yellow face and half shut eyes. He smiled in a very mysterious and superior way as he placed the tray on Mr Salteena's pointed knees.

Here it is rather difficult to know where to begin, because, although the passage is fairly unambiguous in its language, both the social and the literary environment seem to be in a state of disorder. Quite apart from the décor of the room, the behaviour of Procurio is irregular, and so is the interest we are asked to take in him. The author's attention seems to be on details that are usually treated as insignificant. It is something of a relief to learn that she was only 9 years old.[25] In this case the child's imperfect understanding of the adult social environment and of the adult literary environment are combined in a result whose imperfection has the effect of piquing the curiosity of the adult reader. Without the expected norms of the social environment and the literary environment, her unintentionally faulty rendition of them would lose its charm.

Meaning is arrived at by the process of the triangle of literary interpretation, a process in which the author's part is finished when the text is completed.[26] Are there any circumstances in which we would regard authors as superior judges of the meaning of their own texts, supposing that the authors were available to express opinions? We have already considered the very limited extent to which speakers may be considered as privileged judges of the meaning of their own statements. In only three circumstances was their superiority allowed: cases of ambiguous utterance, cases of inadequate definition, and cases of statements that seem to be meaningless. Such cases are more likely to occur in spontaneous, unpremeditated discourse than in works of literature; nevertheless they may occur. But the difference between spontaneous utterance and literary text is a very considerable one and it complicates the issue of authorial authority.

In the first place we may allow that authors may know what they meant by terms that to us seem ambiguous. One might have accepted T. S. Eliot's explanation of what Prufrock's meaning was when he said, 'I shall wear the bottoms of my trousers rolled', but only so long as his explanation could be accommodated to our alternative expectations. Did he mean rolled in the sense of being rolled up as a wader might roll up his trousers, or did he mean rolled in the sense of having cuffs, or had he in mind some way of pressing the trousers? But if one accepted T. S. Eliot's explanation one would also accept the explanation of one of his contemporaries from his own social milieu. One wants to know what the text meant, not what T. S. Eliot meant by the text.

In a case such as ' "Beauty is truth, truth beauty", – that is all / Ye know on earth, and all ye need to know' the definition is inadequate. If we could ask Keats what his lines meant, we might accept his answer as authoritative on the ground that he was completing an incomplete text that had unintentionally been left incomplete. But if his answer seemed to be at odds with our understanding of the rest of his 'Ode on a Grecian Urn' we might want him to argue his case and show how his meaning made sense.

In the case of an utterance that seemed nonsensical or meaningless, the Bastard's 'Philip! sparrow!', for example, in *King John*, Shakespeare's opinion would be of interest, but in the same way that the opinion of a member of his company of players or of a well-informed member of his audience would be. We should be inclined to constrain the credence we gave to an answer within the limited boundaries of certain kinds of expectation.

All of these cases involve decisions about the meaning of utterances, although they are utterances in texts. They are approached by means of the triangle of linguistic interpretation, not the triangle of literary interpretation, and, assuming that author and reader share the same language, the issue is 'situation', which may be private and inadequately communicated. Once one moves to the triangle of literary interpretation, situation is replaced by the combination of social environment and literary environment, both of which are shared. Are there any instances in which an author's view on the overall meaning of a text, or the meaning of a substantial part of a text, is privileged?

One of the difficulties about this question is that it is too general. Neither the answer 'never' nor the answer 'always' is really defensible, and 'sometimes' is scarcely satisfactory even if it is true. By 'author' do we mean all authors? By 'text' do we mean all texts? Usually, when we seek advice we choose our advisers more carefully. Authors may be profound or superficial, careful or careless, self-conscious in their work or instinctive, honest or dishonest, and they may have good memories or bad ones. Questions about authors' right to determine for us what they meant, after the fact, are generally considered in isolation from such practical problems because a general rule is sought. A text may seem to require explanation because it refers to things with which we are not familiar, the author having presumed upon a shared environment that is not in fact shared by others. (The different but related problem of works that have become obscure with the passage of time is discussed in the next chapter.) It may require explanation because it looks at things that are familiar in a way that is so unfamiliar that readers may balk at it, unwilling to believe what it seems to say, or, feeling uncertain about it, seek reassurance. In such cases the text is more private than texts normally are and there may not be a well-informed public to which the puzzled reader can turn.

Apart from the need to discriminate between different kinds of authors and different kinds of texts, and between the kinds of questions of meaning that can usefully be referred to the author, there is an assumption about the relationship of authors to their texts that is widely taken for granted and that complicates the issue. The assumption is that in a work of literature an author is deliberately communicating a point of view or is making a statement. On this assumption it seems reasonable when communication of the point of view or statement is imperfect to turn to the author for clarification if the author is available, making allowance for the passage of time intervening between composition and public reception of the text or between composition and the request for clarification. This assumption is so widespread among modern readers that it may seem quixotic to question it, but because it prejudices discussion of authorial authority it is important that we be aware of its origins and its limitations.[27]

The belief that works of literature typically express an author's views or an author's state of mind is a symptom of the success that literature from the Romantic period onwards has had in presenting itself rhetorically in that guise. What began as a pose on the part of European authors in the later eighteenth century seems gradually to have become a settled conviction in the minds of readers and, perhaps even more surprisingly, in the minds of authors themselves.[28] It may be conceded immediately that there has always been some polemical literature. But its meaning is rarely in doubt, and where uncertainties exist they tend to be taken up by subsequent polemicists and clarified sooner or later. In such literature, in any case, the interest traditionally lay not in what the particular author meant but in what someone arguing a particular case should have meant. It may also be conceded, but with qualification, that the tradition of confessional writing goes back a long way. Confessional writing until the Renaissance seems to have been undertaken with a public in mind and with a wish to reform – the supposition that, say, St Augustine's *Confessions* are a true account of the facts of St Augustine's life (such as they are) is a modern one.[29] Confessional writing from the Renaissance until the later eighteenth century that was not intended for publication consists mainly of diaries kept by people who wished to keep track of their own moral development but who had no thought of sharing the results with others; the confessional writing that was published seems to have been calculated to persuade readers to change their ways (after the example of Augustine) or to alter their views of some public issue or issues. Since the eighteenth century, confessional writing has begun to assume a central place in literature and to be taken for granted as being evidence of the authors' actual lives.

The oddness of the assumption that a text expresses an author's views or state of mind will seem more apparent if one considers it in relation to other forms of creativity. Take, for example, the making of chairs. When we think about a particular chair, even a particular throne, we are accustomed to considering it in terms of its function (to be sat on) and, if it is unusual, in terms of the intended sitter. If it is a chair of Chippendale design we may also think of the designs (chinoiserie, etc.) that prevailed when such chairs were made, associating with it designs in architecture, silver, dress, and so on. Even if the chair in question is known to be the work of Thomas Chippendale the elder in person, we do not customarily think of it as being an expression of his personal point of view – at most, we might be able to recover a statement by him explaining why he thought that broad seats were better or that veneer should only be used in certain circumstances. Why do we not expect chairs to be personal expressions of their makers but insist that poems must be personal expressions of their makers?

One answer might be that the fine arts (literature, music, painting) differ from the applied arts and are conventionally distinguished from them, and the point of the distinction is that the applied arts are 'merely' functional whereas the fine arts are expressive. But this distinction, although it is generally accepted, is also a relatively modern one.[30] It is true that it is more difficult to express personal ideas or feelings through the medium of a chair than through the medium of a poem or a novel, but that is not sufficient reason for supposing that the medium of a poem or a novel is typically employed in order to express personal ideas or feelings. In fact we are accustomed to the idea of functional novels, novels that are written in order to sell or – less crassly – in order to satisfy readers, in which authors deliberately avoid the intrusion of thoughts or feelings that they realize are peculiar to themselves or to a minority to which they belong.

Questioning the necessary presence of personal expression in literary texts is not to deny the existence of personal expression or to underrate its importance in much modern literature, but only to remind us that it is less likely for a work of literature to be the expression of the author's thoughts and feelings than it is for a statement or utterance to be the expression of a speaker's thoughts and feelings. The limits to speakers' authority over the meaning of their utterances apply to authors' authority over the meaning of their texts; further, the likelihood of such questions arising is greatly reduced by the public nature of most texts.

If we could ask Milton whether he was 'of the Devil's party', it would make no more sense to ask him than it would to ask another generally informed member of his society. It is not Milton's secret convictions but the extent to which his representation of Satan would have seemed to his public to be subversively attractive that is relevant to our interest in the meaning of his text.[31] The question that may profitably be put to an author is necessarily much more narrowly defined.

Eudora Welty responded interestingly to a question put to her in connection with her short story 'The Worn Path'. When asked whether an old woman's grandson, on whose behalf a long and difficult journey in the story is undertaken, was already dead, Welty replied that she had not really thought about this question and that her mind when she was writing was on the grandmother's experience rather than on the grandson (pp. 219–21). She concluded that if she had been asked she would have said that the grandson was still alive (the grandmother's journey was not only the result of an inner compulsion), but her uncertainty exemplifies a difference between the point of view of an author and the point of view of a reader that must often exist. Requests for further information or further clarification can often only be met by a new process of creation. The question is akin to asking Shakespeare, 'How many children had Lady Macbeth?'

The appeal to the author is superficially an attractive idea. As we have seen, it is analogous to the appeal made in certain circumstances to a speaker whose utterance is inadequately confirmed. When a literary text is involved, however, the presumption is that it is finished and public; recourse to the author requires a special case to be made for it and even then is severely limited. The closest one can come to a general method of establishing the meaning of a text is the triangle of literary interpretation.

2

DISPLACED ENVIRONMENTS

> The man who reads a work meant for immediate effect on one age, with the notions and feelings of another, may be a refined gentleman, but must be a sorry critic.
>
> S. T. Coleridge

The idea that a past work of literature can survive the passage of time essentially undamaged is consequent upon the general experience that we are often deeply responsive to such works. This deep response seems to owe nothing to critical interference of any kind. Our experience (like the Protestant experience of God with which it may be significantly contemporaneous) is direct, unmediated by the commentary or intercession of experts. We are sure that the old book we have in front of us has remained the same and it is immediately and fundamentally intelligible to us. Anyone who is used to reading criticism will realize that this sureness naïvely overlooks a number of qualifications, but it is a true reflection of the way in which readers usually read and it is the basis upon which most self-conscious kinds of reading are later built. This sense of the presentness of a past work of literature is one of literature's greatest strengths.

Decay is most obvious in the fine arts. Statues lose arms or legs and are admired without them (the *Venus de Milo*) or with speculative repairs (*Laocoön*); frescos are affected by the decay of walls and are crudely overpainted (*The Last Supper*); oil paintings darken under a combination of varnish and urban grime (*The Night Watch*). Attempts are made to restore such works to their original condition, and opinions as to the success of these attempts are often fiercely divided because having the work in one state is incompatible with having it in another. Works of literature can suffer this kind of decay. The unique manuscript of *Beowulf* is a case in point. Having survived intact from the Middle Ages, it was badly scorched in the fire that damaged the library of Sir Robert Cotton in 1731 and has deteriorated further over the years, as charred edges have crumbled to ashes. In 1787 the Danish scholar Thorkelin made a transcript that preserves some of the readings that have since been lost (Thorkelin's transcript narrowly escaped destruction in turn during Nelson's bombardment of Copenhagen in 1801). Differences of opinion about which version to use and about the desirability of repairing the missing portions with hypothetical readings can readily be accommodated by the publication of different versions. Decay of this kind, parallel to the decay that is such a problem to the fine arts, is of minor importance to literature, and instances such as that of the *Beowulf* manuscript are remembered mainly because they are uncharacteristically colourful. Since the invention of printing, works of literature as physical objects have generally survived unscathed.

Literature resists physical decay because, like music, it is only partly complete as a physical object. It requires a reader, a person educated to transform its pages of print into a mental experience. Art also requires the practised co-operation of a beholder,[1] but because literature requires even more of the reader than art requires of the beholder it is physically less vulnerable.[2] The true decay that afflicts literature is invisible; it is within ourselves. In a sense, it is not the objects that have decayed but the readers.

This suggestion may seem nonsensical at first. We do not feel decayed. Mentally and physically we are as well preserved as readers of the past were. When we are fresh from attending a play by Shakespeare or reading a novel by Jane Austen we have no sense of our inadequacy or of being less fully competent readers than we once were. Nevertheless, as readers of past literature we are demonstrably decayed because we do not bring to it the experience that it required for its imaginative or intellectual realization in its own time; instead we bring the experience that is required for the realization of literature in our time, an experience in which only fragments of the earlier experience survive. The consequence is in several respects analogous to the antique statues' loss of limbs.

I

In a sense all works of literature belong to the past; they are a record of past utterances. When we speak of past literature, however, we usually mean literature that emanates from generations previous to our own or, if we are young, literature that existed before we were born. Our sense of its pastness arises from our observation of discrepancies between the world it depicts and the attitudes it conveys and those that are familiar from our own experience of life. Habitual readers usually accommodate themselves to the alien quality of past literature so early in life that they take it for granted. They are more inclined to stress the presentness of past literature and to insist upon the continuing vitality and appositeness of great works. It is in fact perfectly apparent that many past works of literature are as popular and as much part of the shared consciousness of modern readers as any recent works are. It seems reasonable to ask, therefore, in what, if anything, the pastness of past literature consists.

The difference between past literature and contemporary literature may not be immediately evident to casual readers, even though they will usually know which is which, but it becomes more obvious if one applies to it the working of the triangle of literary interpretation as it has been explained in the preceding chapter. The three elements of the triangle, it will be recalled, were the text, the reader, and the environment. When a work of literature is new, the environment of the reader and the environment taken for granted by the text are shared and may be said to be congruent. When the environment is not shared, or is only imperfectly shared (as may be the case when a work written in one country is read by a reader from another), incongruencies are perceived by the reader and misunderstanding is likely. (It is, of course, possible for a text to present incongruencies deliberately, presuming upon the shared environment as a basis for disturbing effects.) With the passage of time, however, the environment to which a text refers remains fixed, while the environment of subsequent generations of readers is subject to change. The effect of such change may not be easy to notice but it is inexorable. Bit by bit a past work of literature will come to refer to one environment while its readers refer to another. This phenomenon may be called the *displacement of environment* and it is the most serious obstacle to understanding what past works of literature meant.[3]

In diagram form the change may be represented in three stages as in figure 4. The partial displacement of environment (stage 2) is likely to distort the experience of reading the text to a more or less severe extent; the complete displacement of environment (stage 3) is likely to lead to readers' experiencing what is essentially a different work or to their being completely baffled, even though the text itself remains the same. The text does not contain a built-in alarm system to warn us of the displacement of environment; indeed, the assumption conveyed by the text that the environment is shared is usually accepted unresistingly by the reader.

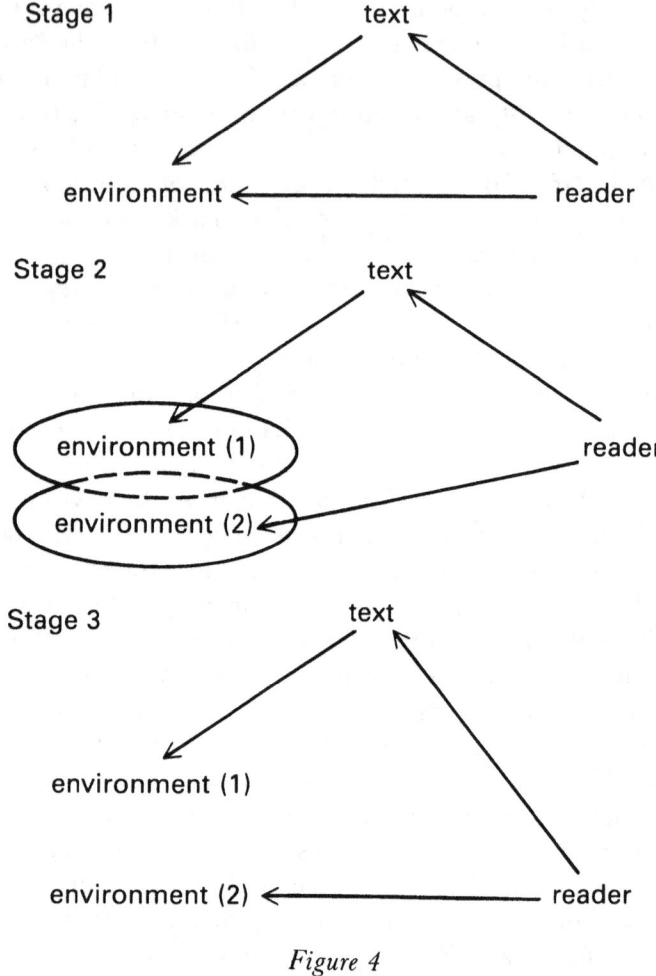

Figure 4

Examples of the misunderstandings that arise from the displacement of environment sometimes enliven the gossip of senior common rooms, but no reader is immune to such mistakes. The stages of displacement may be illustrated simply in the case of readings of Book I of *Gulliver's Travels*. Swift's contemporaries recognized, when they read of the dispute between the proponents of high heels and of low heels, that a reference was being made to Tories and Whigs or the High and Low Church, and, when they read of the division between Big-Endians and Little-Endians, that a reference was being made to Roman Catholics and Protestants. They shared the environment to which the text referred. Well-informed modern readers are aware that political and theological parties are being referred to, although unless they are specialists in the period they are unlikely to have either much sense of the issues involved or much genuine sympathy with the passions they once aroused. Their understanding results from partial displacement of environment (stage 2) with who knows what distortion of the experience that the text once invoked. The naïve modern reader – the child, let us say, to avoid giving offence – will accept the high heels and low heels and the Big-Endians and Little-Endians in the same spirit as he or she accepts the size of the Lilliputians. For such a reader the displacement of environment is complete (stage 3); a political satire has become a fairy-tale.

The example of *Gulliver's Travels* is familiar enough to be dismissed as characteristic of what happens to books written for adults that become classics for children, and because we are used to the idea that the minds of children are not really the equals of our own, especially in matters of judgement, their harmless misreading seems inapplicable to ourselves. However, although it may be true that children are more readily satisfied by a fairy-tale than their elders are, the factor that causes them to read *Gulliver's Travels* as a fairy-tale, displacement of environment, is one against which the adult world has no defence except historical criticism. It seems likely that many other past works of literature are misread by adults as children misread *Gulliver's Travels*.

Another example of misreading with which we are familiar but which seems usually to apply only to others is the misreading that results from encounters with literature in foreign languages. When one visits a foreign country and finds communications difficult there is no temptation to protest that the natives have misunderstood their own language or to claim that one's own version of it is better. One's energies are directed to acquainting oneself with a prevailing norm. When formal instruction is given in foreign languages it is usual to support the new vocabulary, accidence, and sentence structure with basic information about modes of living that differ from one's own and that might cause one to misunderstand or to be misunderstood if they were not taken into account. Beginning with arrangements for travel, provision for food and lodging – the differences which a traveller first encounters – and moving on to institutions, laws, customs, proverbs, and idioms, the students are artificially and rapidly apprised of an environment that differs from their own by being made aware of the differences and attaching them at first consciously but in the end habitually to the environment in which they have grown up. This process is a demanding one, and its results even for gifted and resolutely industrious students are never comparable to the acquaintance with environment one has learned first in one's own language. It is less detailed, it does not play a part in forming the mind, and it is less reliable. Even after years of living in a foreign-language country it is possible to feel that one is acting a role rather than simply being oneself. The language difference makes us accept this situation; the changed environment seems to be merely symptomatic of it. However, although language and environment are interdependent, the problem of a strange environment is separable from the problem of a strange language. It is just that the problem of the strange language makes us more observant, less confident of our own assumptions, and more inclined to take a positive interest in the possibility that another society thinks and behaves differently from our own, and that it takes for granted experiences and surroundings that differ from our own.

The difference between the environment of the English-speaking world and, say, the French-speaking world is considerable, and it is possible to spend a lifetime trying to become as adept in one as in the other. Most English speakers are content to carry the effort to the point where they can function in the French environment without being a public nuisance but do not expect to be taken for natives of it. The difference between the environment of the twentieth century and the nineteenth century, however, is infinitely greater than the difference between the environments of any modern western countries. The only reason we are not more strongly aware of the difference is that we do not have to attempt to live in the nineteenth century and that the similarity of language conceals from us the difference in the environment referred to. As one goes back further in time, the differences in environment become more and more drastic and less and less predictable.

Take, for example, the following description of the eccentric but benevolent Mr Dick in *David Copperfield* (chapter 17):

> He was a universal favourite, and his ingenuity in little things was transcendent. He could cut oranges into such devices as none of us had an idea of. He could make a boat out of anything, from a skewer upwards. He could turn crampbones into chessmen; fashion

Roman chariots from old court cards; make spoked wheels out of cotton reels, and birdcages of old wire. But he was greatest of all, perhaps, in the articles of string and straw; with which we were all persuaded he could do anything that could be done by hands.

What do we make of such an account? Allowing for the fact that we are being given David's childhood reminiscence and that a considerable element of archness is present in this section of the novel, what is it that Mr Dick is doing? The answer, for most readers, will be that he improvises toys for children out of unexpectedly commonplace materials. This answer is true, but what an impoverishment it is of the original! If one looks at the details of the passage it is apparent that more particular questions could be asked. How does one cut an orange into 'devices'? What sort of devices are they? How can a boat be made out of a skewer? What sort of a skewer is meant? What sort of boat? What is a crampbone, and is it like or unlike a chessman? What sort of a chessman is to be imagined? How does one fashion a Roman chariot from old court cards, and are court cards used because of their figures or their colours or what? What sort of cotton reels can be made into spoked wheels? What is meant by 'articles of string or straw'? Such questions put to a group of modern readers will produce a range of answers that might suggest that readers' experiences of *David Copperfield* vary greatly, but most readers never ask these questions. They grasp the gist of the passage and hurry happily on. If one were allowed to translate foreign languages in this way, their study would be made considerably easier. The experience of modern readers in reading *David Copperfield*, if they are content with the general meaning of the details of an environment that is foreign to their experience, is radically different from the experience of readers contemporary with Dickens. The displacement of environment results in the experience of a different work of literature, even though the text remains the same.

It may be objected that descriptive detail of the kind just considered is subject to the erosion of time in a way that the essential meaning of a work is not. This is a very dubious proposition. Descriptive detail is certainly easier to point to by way of illustrating the decay of meaning, and modern readers who are challenged to make sense of details in their favourite old texts will usually be obliged to concede that they are satisfied with only a general or vague comprehension of matter which was once perfectly obvious. But the same sort of difficulty arises with the central experiences of past works of literature. Take, for example, the death of little Nell in *The Old Curiosity Shop* – so heart-rending to Victorian readers and so much less interesting to most of us. The discrepancy in response is sometimes put down to the excessive sentimentality of the Victorians, or to our having better objects on which to lavish our sympathies, but the displacement of environment that forces us to have an experience that differs very greatly from the Victorian experience is surely a factor. The effect of displacement of environment over the whole length of a novel is too large to be brought forward conveniently as evidence, but if one multiplies the paragraph on Mr Dick by, let us say, a thousand some idea may be gathered of the scale of likely distortion.[4]

The effects of displacement of environment are of three types. The most obvious and the one most likely to result in total misunderstanding is the kind displayed by the example of *Gulliver's Travels*. The second involves the ignoring of detail that does not make sense, the one shown in the description of Mr Dick. Its effect is to impoverish a work, to reduce it to a longwinded summary of itself. The third is a consequence of the second, as in the example of little Nell, and it may deprive us of the basis necessary for sympathy with characters or with action, or may even cause us (as in the case of Shylock in *The Merchant of Venice* or Satan in *Paradise Lost*) to invest with sympathy characters who in their original environment would have been refused it.

This situation is further complicated by the variousness of past environments. For, while the past and present may be weighed against one another as being competing or conflicting or merely different environments in terms of the experience of an individual or of a generation, the past itself is made up of a long sequence of changing environments in which many differ as much from one another (the fifth century from the eighteenth, say) as the more recent ones (the nineteenth century, say) differ from our own. The difficulties caused by the variety of past environments is usefully exhibited by the historical novel (and prior to it by epics and romances).

Scott's *Heart of Midlothian*, for example, was written in the early nineteenth century but describes events, some real and some imaginary, that are set in the middle of the eighteenth century. Because the historical novel was a relatively new genre, Scott was careful to make the eighteenth-century environment explicit.[5] He directed the attention of his readers to significant differences between the past environment and their own environment; he 'reminded' his readers of customs and events of which they and their parents and grandparents must have had only vague recollections. For the nineteenth-century reader, interpretation of this novel was reasonably straightforward. It may be represented diagrammatically as in figure 5. The reader read the novel with two environments in mind, the past environment (the eighteenth-century one) being provided where needed by the text, and the text referred to two environments (the present and the past), often, presumably, taking one environment (the present) for granted while referring to the other (the past).

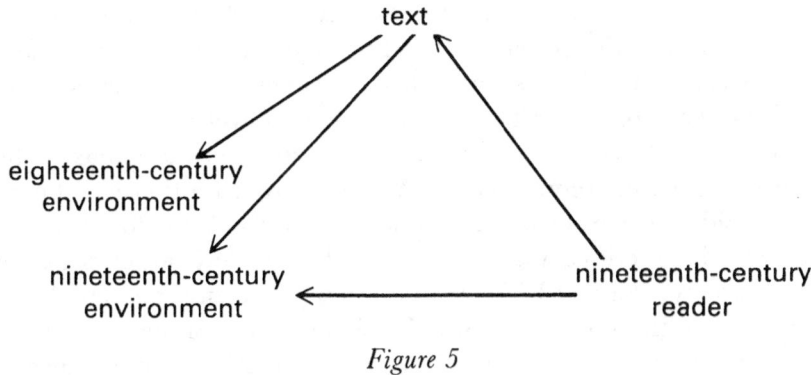

Figure 5

When such a novel is read in the twentieth century the unavoidable displacement of the nineteenth-century environment by our twentieth-century one affects our understanding both of the nineteenth-century environment and of the eighteenth-century environment to which the novel addresses itself. One is inclined to assume that, although the present of a work of literature will become the past of future readers, its past will remain the past. However, the past is always described in terms of the present (the unfamiliar being explained necessarily in terms of the familiar), and with the passage of time the past of the present will become the past of the past and not the past of the present. This state of affairs may be represented diagrammatically as in figure 6.

A modern reader may be knowledgeable about the eighteenth century, just as Scott himself was, and may be able to supplement the account given of it in the novel. This procedure may do something to

46   HISTORICAL CRITICISM AND THE MEANING OF TEXTS

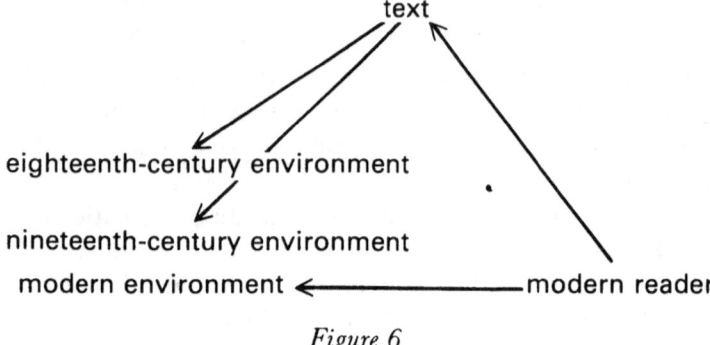

Figure 6

compensate for details that Scott left out on the assumption that his (nineteenth-century) readers already knew them; it may also add details of which he was unaware and correct details about which subsequent knowledge has shown him to have been misinformed. But the experience of this small class of readers too is different from the experience of the original readers of the novel.

The case of science fiction or of utopian literature makes the nature of this difference clearer. A utopia by definition is fictional and outside the experience of anyone. In More's *Utopia*, for example, a society is described that never existed and the characteristics of which are determined by their relevance to the environment More shared with his contemporaries. The book is not strong on realistic detail, including just enough to give it the superficial appearance of travel literature, and when it takes up such matters as government, international affairs, and economics, or marriage, religious beliefs, and methods of employment, it does so on the assumption that the utopian practices will be compared with those that prevailed in the environment of the reader, the environment of early sixteenth-century England. The diagrammatic representation of the experience of the original readers of *Utopia*, shown in figure 7, would be similar to the representation of the experience of the original readers of *Heart of Midlothian* (see figure 5), but reference to the sixteenth-century environment is implicit and not explicit. Diagrammatic representation of the modern reader's experience, shown in figure 8, follows the same pattern as the representation of the modern reader's experience of *Heart of Midlothian* (see figure 6). With *Utopia* as well the readers' environment is a displaced one, leaving them uncertain as to what is ironical or humorous and obliging them to read to some extent like the child readers of *Gulliver's Travels*,

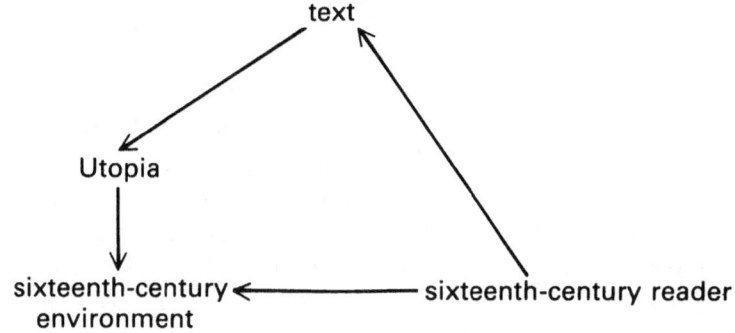

Figure 7

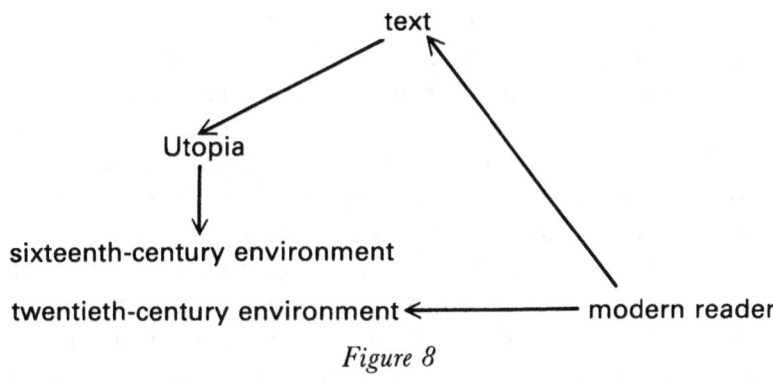

Figure 8

unaware of much that the text takes for granted. However, while the diagram resembles the diagram for *Heart of Midlothian* in several respects, there is no temptation or opportunity for modern readers to supplement their ignorance of sixteenth-century assumptions about Utopia with twentieth-century knowledge as there is to supplement their ignorance of nineteenth-century assumptions about the eighteenth century with twentieth-century ones. This difference may suggest the hazards of even the best-informed efforts to read historical fiction in the light of modern knowledge of the historical period referred to; it is likely not only to differ substantially from the historical knowledge presumed by the fiction itself but to interfere with it, producing different emphases in ways that would be difficult even to guess at. The only safe route to understanding nineteenth-century representations of the eighteenth-century environment is through the nineteenth-century environment.[6]

II

The effect of the passage of time on the environment has been discussed so far in this chapter in terms of the social environment. But the literary environment is also subject to gradual change and while this change is, perhaps, less noticeable it too causes a displacement of environment in the triangle of interpretation.

The most obviously vulnerable aspect of the literary environment and the one that resembles the social environment most closely is popular contemporary literature. It is usual for us to read widely and even promiscuously in the writing of our own time, including periodicals and bestsellers of all kinds, to attend plays and films and to watch television with no aim other than gratification. We are not much concerned to find that our tastes differ from the tastes of others, and we do not feel particularly anxious about repairing accidental omissions. At the same time we are made aware that certain books or films are popular and may well be led out of curiosity to see whether we enjoy them too. Each year the newspapers provide us with charts of the most popular books, films, records, and so on. Prizes are handed out and literary reputations are made. In conversation a familiarity with currently popular forms of art is taken for granted, and one has only to move from one country to another to be reminded how much casual communication depends upon an acquaintance with the prevailing popular hits. Authors generally share this acquaintance and assume that their readers share it too. This assumption need not be conscious; it would, in fact, require an effort not to make it.

While we maintain a relatively effortless and pleasurable acquaintance with current literature, we do not expect that much of it will continue to interest us in years to come. If we are interested in such predictions we may maintain that certain works are more likely to have staying power than others, but we do not have to be particularly well informed to know that such predictions usually fare no better than predictions about the future of the stock market. Because we take our acquaintance with current literature for granted, just as we take for granted the social environment, we do not often take the trouble to comment on it. A few works will continue to be read and, as long as they are, references to them will continue to be recognized. For the most part, popular contemporary literature, like popular literature in the past, will be forgotten.

The effect of this loss on contemporary works of literature is in some ways even more damaging to the interpretation of literature than the change of social environment. In diagrammatic form it may be represented as in figure 9. The diagram of displacement of literary environment looks very much like the earlier diagram (figure 5 above) of the displacement of social environment. In one respect, literary form or genre, what it represents really is similar. The modern reader who reads Sidney's *Arcadia* with the novels of Iris Murdoch in mind will certainly be puzzled and surprised at times by differences between the conventions of the romance and the conventions of the modern novel, but the differences of form draw attention to themselves and if one pauses over them can generally be explained. At the level of reference to particular works, however, the modern reader is often simply unaware of reference to literature contemporary with Sidney. Here the parallel might be to naïve reading of *Gulliver's Travels*: irony or satire degenerate into fairy-tale; the portrait or caricature that outlives its subject can no longer interest us by its likeness.

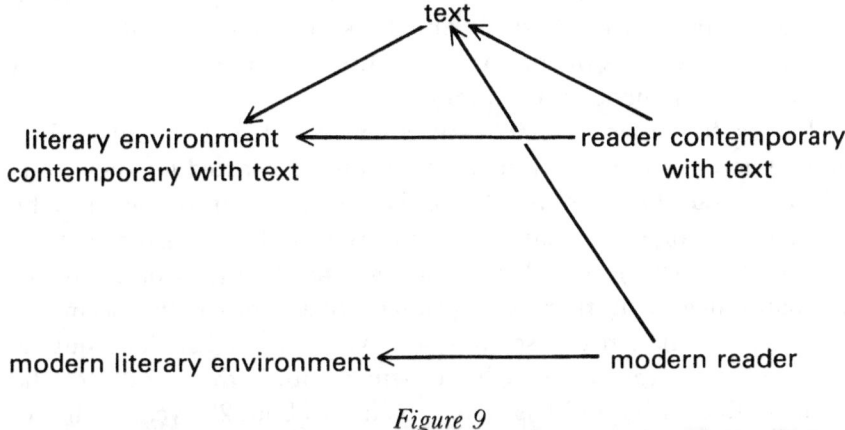

Figure 9

The presence of ephemeral literature in the literary environment is illustrated by Jane Austen's *Mansfield Park* of 1814, in which an amateur performance of Mrs Inchbald's play *Lovers' Vows* is rehearsed. Modern readers have neither seen nor read *Lovers' Vows*, but when Austen wrote the novel the play was the most popular one in London. It could be taken for granted that readers would have seen or read it.[7] Now, however, ignorance of *Lovers' Vows* has become an obstacle to readers, subjecting them to intrusive footnotes and to the distraction of appendices, and altering the experience of reading the novel almost beyond recognition. By contrast, O'Keeffe's roughly contemporary comedy *Wild Oats* of 1791, in which a group of travelling actors perform *Twelfth Night* in company with some amateurs at a country house, has been revived successfully for modern audiences because the part of the literary environment referred to (Shakespeare's play) happens not to have been ephemeral.

It must be conceded, however, that the literary environment of current ephemera is a more important element in some works of literature than in others. Satire and polemical writing are notoriously vulnerable to the decay of both their social and their literary environments, and only extraordinary excellence, some of which is evident in spite of the decay, has warranted the recovery operations undertaken on behalf of Dryden, Pope, and Swift. With the exception of these works it might be hoped that the literary environment would differ from the social environment because the books survive unchanged while society is steadily altered. Is there not, after all, a fairly stable canon of great works that have long been taken for granted by readers and writers alike? Homer, Virgil, Shakespeare, Milton, Wordsworth, Dickens are the sort of names that come to mind. But even this major part of the literary environment can be a treacherous element in interpretation.

In the first place the literary environment gives a misleading impression of stability. Homer, to be sure, has lasted for thousands of years, but between the barbarian invasion of Rome and the Renaissance one finds hardly any awareness of the existence of the *Iliad* or the *Odyssey*, and there is no sign that literary works took an acquaintance with them for granted. Shakespeare too seems to represent permanence in so far as any writer in English does, but his pre-eminence was not widely recognized until the middle of the eighteenth century and has lasted so far for about 250 years. That in itself may seem a sufficient guarantee of permanence, barring further barbarian catastrophes, but there is the troubling precedent of Chaucer's contemporary, John Gower, whose *Confessio Amantis* ranked alongside *The Canterbury Tales* and *Troilus and Criseyde* for 300 years and then sank into oblivion. 'Length of duration and continuance of esteem' may, as Samuel Johnson suggested, be our best guide to literary excellence, but as he acknowledged it is an imperfect one.

Its imperfections are camouflaged to some extent by our habit of referring to works of literature by their authors' names rather than by the titles of the works themselves. The sustained popularity of Shakespeare cannot be equated with the sustained popularity of *Coriolanus*, for example, or of *Henry VIII*, although both these plays have had their day in the sun and it was once possible for an author to take for granted our recollections of empathy with Volumnia or Wolsey. The Wordsworth now familiar to us from *The Prelude* was venerated by Shelley, Keats, Arnold, and Tennyson for *The Excursion*. In our own time interest in Byron has shifted dramatically from *Childe Harold's Pilgrimage* to *Don Juan*.

Even when the works remain the same, the experience of reading them is rarely stable. When Samuel Pepys says of *Macbeth* (in his *Diary* for 19 April 1667) that 'it is one of the best plays for a stage, and variety of dancing and music, that ever I saw', we realize that the production he had seen must have differed from those we are used to and we make allowance for that difference. When we read about the consternation caused by the decision of Mrs Siddons to set down her candlestick in order to be able to go through the motions of washing her hands in the sleepwalking scene, we are made aware of a focus of familiarity in *Macbeth* that differs appreciably from our own without being seriously at odds with it. The need felt from the end of the seventeenth century to the beginning of the nineteenth to perform *King Lear* with a happy ending is symptomatic of an empathy with the plight of Lear and Cordelia that exceeds our own in its unguardedness; Shakespeare's bleak conclusion was unbearable.[8] These examples of changes in taste are familiar to students of Shakespeare's reputation and might readily be multiplied; they have a special importance, however, when one is trying to assess the stability of the literary environment. It is not enough for us to recognize a literary allusion; if we do not respond to the work alluded to in roughly the same way as the original readers, we may still understand the force of the allusion quite differently.

One of the better-known examples of this sort of problem is the changing view of Milton's Satan in *Paradise Lost*. Blake was of the opinion that Milton was 'of the Devil's party without knowing it', and this view of Satan as heroic in the face of overwhelming odds and of Milton's God as a complacent prig seems to predominate among readers over the past 200 years. At the same time modern Miltonists have been at pains to point out that neither Milton nor his contemporaries shared this view; the interpretation of *Paradise Lost* demonstrably changed during the later eighteenth century.[9] The situation that would arise for a Romantic reader if Satan were referred to in a work of literature of the early eighteenth century may be represented diagrammatically as in figure 10. The allusion to Satan in the text would be to the character in *Paradise Lost* (1) who is noted for spiritual pride and vindictiveness; the allusion would be taken by the Romantic reader to be to the character in *Paradise Lost* (2) who is noted for stoical and stubborn resistance to tyranny. The displacement of the literary environment here is one caused by changes in the interpretation of the works of which it is composed. These changes in turn may be caused in part by changes in the social environment (the rise of individualism, the challenge to authoritarian rule, and the currency of revolution all coincide with the changed view of Satan) or by changes in the literary environment (greater stress was being laid on sympathy and less on intellectual consistency), but however they arise they prevent the literary environment from being spared the ravages of time. It is sheer luck that we are able to appreciate Partridge's reactions to *Hamlet* in *Tom Jones*; Fielding might just as well have had him attend a performance of *King John*, for Garrick was performing in both plays in 1745.

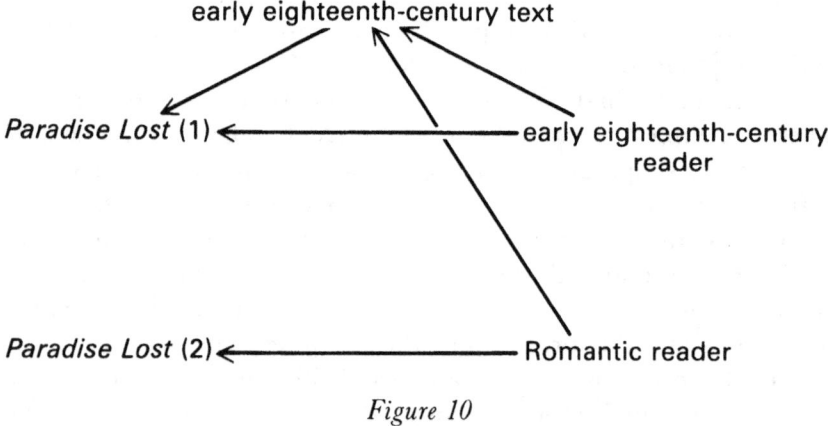

Figure 10

III

Criticism has not had to wait for a display of diagrams to be aware of the effects of the displacement of environment. The effects have always been obvious to those who knew more about past environments than most of their contemporaries. Well-read critics have been able to protect the common reader from historical misreadings by tactfully anticipating them and heading them off; and teachers, whose students are a constant reminder of the accident-proneness as well as of the freshness of the innocent eye, have accumulated the most obvious of these tactful headings-off as footnotes in undergraduate anthologies. In Witherspoon and Warnke's old standby, *Seventeenth-Century Prose and Poetry*, the 'vegetable' of 'vegetable love' in Marvell's 'To His Coy Mistress' is helpfully labelled 'growing in the manner of plants', to ward off incongruous thoughts of a passion for carrots and cabbages. In *The Norton Anthology of English Literature*, fervid misunderstandings of Donne's 'The Ecstasy' are firmly suppressed with the advice that 'For Donne's readers the word "ecstasy" implied, not wild delight, as it commonly does nowadays, but a standing apart, a movement of the soul outside of the body.'

The impulse behind such notes is sound enough. Instructors who have noticed that their students regularly 'misread' particular words in favourite set texts provide the equivalent for them of the glossaries supplied for Middle English texts or of the vocabularies included in elementary anthologies in foreign languages. As an instructional device the well-placed footnote is realistic and useful. It provides the necessary orientation for the literary novice. But as a norm for critical practice it sets a worrying precedent. In the first place it is a short-cut. How do editors of texts know that the words they annotate did not mean once what they mean today? And if the editor in turn, as one suspects is increasingly the case, relies upon the knowledge of yet another annotator, perhaps even one of an earlier generation, how did the original annotator know? The answer is that the original annotator was widely read in literature contemporary with the work in question. This kind of knowledge is not only preferable to the next best thing, appeal to old dictionaries; it is akin to the knowledge on which old dictionaries were based. The difference between knowing what a word or a passage means in this manner and knowing it because one has been told what it means by some critical authority is the difference between living reading – the kind we experience when we read the literature of our own time – and dead reading – reading as a form of academic exercise. The contrast between the two is so great and so obvious that it is to be feared that many readers simply give up the literature of the past as a lost cause.

The question is ultimately one not of meaning itself but of the way in which meaning is arrived at. If, as we have seen, the triangle of interpretation is made up of text, environment, and reader, the effect of reliance on explanatory notes is to pretend that the displacement of environment may be compensated for by an absence of environment. The meal is indigestible to the inexperienced stomach, so we serve it pre-digested. The reader's most basic instincts are attacked by this procedure. If some words do not mean what they mean in everyday life, perhaps no words mean what they mean in everyday life. The reading of literature is reduced, fatally, to a game in which anything goes. One cannot learn to read 'To His Coy Mistress' or 'The Ecstasy' by this method; the most that one can do is be guided through the crude outlines of the previous reading done by an editor or instructor. Some students, among them good readers, rebel against this kind of force-feeding, sensing its artificiality even if they cannot quite explain it; the more docile learn what they are told and gradually build up a vocabulary of such notes until the time comes for them to pass their 'readings' on to yet another generation.

But even the docile, many of whom are also good readers, notice that something is missing. The need for annotated texts narrows the range of texts that are read. The narrower the range the more often the same texts (already pre-digested) have to be read, especially by critics and instructors. It is hardly surprising that texts that once occupied the best thoughts of the New Critics should gradually become impervious to further applications of their methods. And when their texts are disfigured by accompanying explanatory footnotes the experience of reading bears little relation to the experience of reading modern works. It has been noticed by Lukács that realist fiction carries its meaning with it, by what he calls the principle of 'exemplification', comparatively invulnerable to what I have called the displacement of environment, and this may be why young readers are more often captivated by the novel than by poetry. The experience of reading the novels of Defoe or Richardson is felt to be a variation on reading the novels of our own time; the experience of reading the metaphysical poets is *sui generis*. Faced with this unsatisfactory experience, readers have turned to the genuine experience that is left, the relationship of their reading of the past work of literature to themselves. The psychology of reading, the social implications of reading, the relationship of one text unsatisfyingly read to another text unsatisfyingly read – all of these are experienced at first hand, to all of these each of us can contribute without feeling oppressed by the condescending dead hand of historical information.

In the meantime, the texts become subject to a critical law of increasing inertness. Each time a word or a phrase is understood by means of a gloss, the normal experience of reading is interrupted. After repeated readings the gloss is learned and the interruption is no longer noticed; however, the experience of reading is still not normal. An artificial substitute has replaced environment in the triangle of interpretation. When people lose arms or legs these can sometimes be replaced by artificial limbs which permit their wearers to continue doing many of the things that they would otherwise have had to give up doing. But neither they nor those who observe them are in any doubt that the artificial substitutes are only substitutes. The trouble with artificial substitutes for environment in the triangle of interpretation is that there is no prior experience of the real thing against which the substitute can be compared. Human beings can only survive having a certain number of their parts replaced by artificial substitutes, and the same is true of works of literature. With each substitution the life of the work is reduced, its inertness increases, and it gradually becomes moribund. When they are in this state it is only natural to neglect them.

When the energies of the critic are diverted away from texts to 'contexts', the texts remain a shared point of reference. We may talk about the Oedipus complex or about the feminist perspective of Ophelia but we take *Hamlet* for granted. The difficulty here is that, however lively the topic or approach to a text may be, if the text itself is fixed and lifeless it may serve as an illustration or example but is itself unlikely to be illuminated. Further, because it is lifeless, liberties will be taken with it; it will be reduced to a bare caricature of itself – '*Hamlet*, the play about a man who could not make up his mind'. As memories of what it was like to read past works without notes but with a substantial acquaintance with other past works fade and become rarer, sensitive readers who have had little experience of it feel the need to infuse new life into old texts. They will raise questions about the aims of the historical critic.

However, while it is incontestable that the passage of time causes a displacement of both the social environment and the literary environment in the triangle of interpretation and that as a consequence the experience of the modern reader of a work of literature of the past differs from the experience of the readers for whom the work was contemporary, is this matter for regret? Is there not something to be said for conceding the change and being content to respond to the work as it now appears without concerning ourselves with what it once was?[10]

This question is more difficult to answer than it may at first appear to be because the circumstances that surround works of literature are so various. In the case of primitive epics (the *Iliad* and th *Odyssey*) for example, their social and literary environments are unknown and may be irrecoverable. Attempts to reconstruct the environments of these works are largely dependent on the works themselves, and there are major uncertainties about the dates at which they were composed. Primitive epics are a recognized exception. They have established themselves over long periods of time as being of special merit, and they have become an integral part of the literary environment that followed them, serving as models and as yardsticks for subsequent writers and critics. It is even possible that they owe some of their success to being the sole survivors of an otherwise lost civilization and that what we admire in them is not merely a literary quality but the coherence of values and feelings of the whole civilization that they reflect when they take them for granted.

Much effort has gone into trying to learn about the civilization of Homer, but it does not seem to have had much effect on our understanding of his poem. Would we welcome such an effect even from the point of view of historical criticism? We have learned that the Parthenon was once brightly painted, but would we wish to restore it to its original state? The Parthenon has found an apparently secure place in our canon of architectural beauty in its uncoloured, and indeed ruinous, condition. It is quite possible that if it had been perfectly preserved it would nevertheless have been admired as it has been or perhaps even more, but we cannot be sure. What we can be sure of is that it has been admired for several centuries in a form that differed from its original and that it is the decayed, altered version that has shown staying power as an object of aesthetic appreciation. In its decayed state it vies with St Peter's in Rome or St Paul's in London but unlike those more recent buildings it is a mixture of art and accident and is admired in somewhat the way an *objet trouvé* is. The justification for continuing to pay attention to its unpainted form is partly that for several centuries it has been regarded as consummately beautiful and because the architecture and sculpture of several centuries have used it in its decayed state as a model. The historically false version has been woven into the fabric of subsequent art and has acquired an important place in the history of art.

Modern critics of the Parthenon, however, need no longer be 'ignorant' in the way in which eighteenth-century enthusiasts were. Instead they have a choice of roles available to them. If they restrict their activities to such issues as the effect of the unpainted stone on us (the social dimension) or the nature of ideal beauty (the metaphysical dimension), the uninformed view will still serve. If, on the other hand, they wish to comment on such issues as the original meaning or wish to understand the internal coherence of the building (why it made sense to build it in one way rather than in another, what assumptions it made about light, how it was used when it was new, etc.), all the awareness they can muster of the ways in which its present condition differs from its original condition will help them to avoid speculation that is based on misinformation. The choice here is not a choice between good criticism and bad criticism, but rather between criticism that has one kind of aim and criticism that has another kind of aim. As long as readers have some way of telling which is which at the outset, they too can make their choice of the one they are looking for.

The rise of enthusiasm for unpainted classical stonework may be regarded as stemming from an accident of ignorance; a related critical phenomenon that lasted for even longer, the Christian allegorical interpretation of pre-Christian literature, was perfectly deliberate. It is usual to point to St Augustine's exposition of the method involved and the reasoning that lay behind it in his *De Doctrina Christiana*, a work that is devoted to showing how the Christian reader should interpret the Bible. In it he explains that the Old Testament is to be understood in terms of the New Testament and that where it seems not to make literal sense it is to be interpreted figuratively as a foreshadowing of the New Testament. Further, profane literature written prior to the coming of Christ is to be interpreted similarly, on the pretext that 'wherever [the Christian] may find truth, it is his Lord's' (book I, section 18).

Perhaps the most extreme form of this kind of interpretation was the allegorization of Ovid's *Metamorphoses* in the fourteenth century. The authors of these allegorizations were aware that they were treating a pre-Christian work, but they seem to have believed that, if a useful Christian sense could be developed that was consistent with a work of literature that without such a meaning might be useless or even harmful, their efforts would be worthwhile. Accordingly the metamorphosis of Daphne into a laurel tree when she is pursued by Apollo is taken to represent the love of God for the Virgin Mary; Apollo's crowning himself with the laurel is taken to signify God's way of enclosing himself in the body of the woman who will become his mother; Actaeon becomes the crucified Christ and Diana the Trinity that has been seen unclothed by the son of God, and so on.[11] Readings of this sort are familiar from biblical typology; however, whereas in the case of the Bible it was possible to argue that, since it was God's word and since God had foreknowledge, it was reasonable to regard the Old Testament anticipations of New Testament events as being deliberate, the pagan literature of Greece and Rome was annexed in a more imperial spirit.[12]

Modern students of Ovid do not usually regard the medieval allegorizations of their author as a helpful guide to the meaning of his work – indeed, it is possible to study Ovid without really being aware of the existence of the allegorizations. They have, nevertheless, a claim to our attention as literary adaptations in their own right, and ones that enjoyed a reasonably prolonged currency among sophisticated readers. The precedent is useful in its implication that interpretation may be regarded either as the servant of the work being interpreted, to be judged by its reliableness as a guide to what the work once meant, or as a work of literature whose worth is independent of the accuracy of its rendering of the work that it professes to explain.

In the world of art criticism there is a widespread disapproval of what are popularly called fakes, copies of originals that pass themselves off as the real thing. Part of this disapproval is the result of the difference in market value involved, but the difference in market value is in turn the result of the belief that originals are better than copies. Experts have been fooled by fakes since time immemorial, and such errors are part of the lore that laymen cherish as a defence against people with pretensions to being better informed. The failure of the experts does suggest that whatever it is that they appreciate in the original is not missing in the copy. And if a fake escapes detection for long enough, like the statue of the Etruscan soldier at the Metropolitan Museum in New York City let us say, it may have developed a following that would have been denied it if it had been exhibited first as a twentieth-century statue intended to exhibit an

Etruscan spirit.[13] The possibility that a copy may be better than its original is sometimes considered. Again an expert or an art critic may give an opinion on a particular example; but while such an opinion may be persuasive it differs from the 'opinion' expressed by centuries of viewers. The example is perhaps clearer if one considers a free imitation rather than an almost indistinguishable copy. For us to accept the importance of the imitation, it is required to win its way over a period of time.

The literary equivalent of the rival claims of original and imitation is familiar in our own time from the adaptation of old plays and films. The criterion here seems to be one of simple preference. If the new version is better, we not only prefer it, we forget about the old one. If, however, the work being adapted is one that has attained the status of a classic, resistance is likely to come from those who know the original, ostensibly on the ground that the original was better, but sometimes perhaps on the more subjective (though perfectly respectable) ground that the original is valued and familiar and ought not to be jeopardized.

But adaptation is to be found throughout the history of literature; indeed, in a sense, it is what makes it possible for literature to have a history. A number of Shakespeare's plays, for example, are adaptations of previous plays. Not only have his adaptations come to be thought of as models in their own right, but their originals have for the most part been lost to view.[14] We may search for the remains of *Ur-Hamlets* and earlier versions of *King Lear*, but we do so only because we are interested in learning more about Shakespeare's plays (which parts he added, what he was omitting, the tendency and effect of his alterations) and not because we expect to revive the originals as potential rivals to their Shakespearian successors. The reason for this attitude is that Shakespeare's plays have established themselves over time – readers and audiences have agreed that they are excellent. The issue here is not which version was first but which one has succeeded.

The interpretation of literature has two distinguishable aims. They are not necessarily incompatible with one another, but they are not necessarily allied either. One aim is to provide readers with a 'correct' understanding of the work; the other aim is to provide readers with an understanding of the work that is more satisfying or pleasing than their previous understanding or that is satisfying or pleasing in a different way. The success of the first of these aims is judged in terms of the work being interpreted; the success of the second aim is judged in terms of the aesthetic effectiveness of the interpretation.

We have considered three sorts of interpretation – the unpainted Parthenon, the Christian allegorization of pre-Christian literature, the adaptation of plays by Shakespeare – all of which may be said to belong to the second category. We judge them not as accurate renditions of the works in their original form because we know them to be inaccurate; if we value them at all – and most of us value at least the first and third – it is because they are aesthetically[15] pleasing in their own right. This distinction has nothing to do with interpreters' intentions or awarenesses – they may or may not be well informed about the works they are interpreting; it has to do instead with our awareness of the quality and kind of their information. A late medieval interpreter of Ovid who did not know that the poet lived before the Christian era might suppose that the allegorical interpretation was both aesthetically pleasing and true to the original work. With the advantage of better information we can reject the claim to have been true to the original work and nevertheless consider the possibility that the interpretation is aesthetically interesting in the same way that we consider Shakespeare's plays to be aesthetically interesting.

In certain areas of our cultural life the distinction is commonplace. One hears, for example, of a 'Directors' Theatre', that is, of performances of plays in which the interpretation of the director and not the play itself is the object of interest. One may attend a performance of Peter Brook's *Carmen* of 1981, for example, and judge it without reference to the opera by Bizet upon which it is based. It is offered – or it may at any rate be received – as an operatic work and judged to be successful or unsuccessful. If it comes to replace Bizet's *Carmen* of 1875 or if it maintains a secure existence alongside it, it will have been judged to be successful. It is also possible to attend a performance of Brook's *Carmen* and to judge it as an interpretation of Bizet's opera. This criterion is not determined by the director, although he may reveal to us what he thinks we ought to expect. In judging the interpretation offered by its truth to Bizet's opera we compare it to our previous experiences of the opera and our knowledge about it; the more experience and knowledge we have, the more demanding our standard is likely to be. We shall ask ourselves – perhaps after the performance is over – whether the production is true to the original, and, if it takes freedoms, whether these improve our understanding of the original. If not, we are likely to conclude that as an interpretation of the original it has failed.

One hears complaints about 'Directors' Theatre' just as one previously heard complaints about 'Actors' Theatre', and one hears complaints of a related kind about the free interpretations of music offered by conductors and soloists. Such complaints are based on the assumption that the performance is to be judged by its truth to the original effect of the work.[16] If the performance were judged as a new work the criterion would be differently applied. In that case we should ask whether it is better than the old.

The same distinction holds in modern criticism. If there is a 'Directors' Theatre', there seems also to be a 'Critics' Literature'. In the interesting dispute that took place in France in the 1960s between Roland Barthes and Raymond Picard over the merits of Barthes's interpretation of Racine, the issues were confused to some extent by the failure of both disputants to distinguish between two different kinds of interpretative activity.[17] The first kind – the attempt to provide readers with a better understanding of the original effect of the work when it was new – was taken for granted by Picard, who asserted that judged by that criterion Barthes had failed. Barthes responded to this argument by asserting that he not only did not attempt to understand the effect of the work when it was new – and regarded such attempts as illusory – but wished instead to provide readers with an understanding of the work that was more pleasing or satisfying than their previous understanding. Barthes's intentions, however, are not the criterion of his success as far as his readers are concerned. Whether he has or has not improved our understanding of Racine's plays when they first appeared will depend in part on our own previous knowledge and experience of them; whether his interpretation of them is more pleasing or satisfying than our previous understanding will also depend in part on our own previous knowledge and experience.

The importance of displaced environment in this dispute depends upon our awareness of it. If, as in the case of the primitive epic, we have no access to the displaced environment, the decision of an interpreter to ignore it will not have a detectable or assessable effect on our sense of the accuracy of that interpretation. (We should probably draw the line, however, at an interpretation that suggested that the failure of the Greeks in the *Iliad* to demolish the walls of

Troy with siege artillery implied an unconscious wish to fulfil the prophecy that the siege would last for ten years – even if the environment of the primitive epic is largely beyond recovery, it is distinguishable from our own to the extent of lacking cannons and mortars.) If as medieval readers of the allegorization of the *Metamorphoses* we were unaware of the displaced environment of Ovid's time, again we should not find our knowledge of that environment clashing with the environment assumed by the interpreter. If, on the other hand, an interpretation is offered which is demonstrably based on an assumed environment that is in conflict with our knowledge of the displaced environment and which depends upon that assumed environment in order to make its case, we are likely to feel that it has not made its case. Its usefulness as comment on the original work will be dismissed; its usefulness, if any, will be in the creation of a new aesthetically pleasing work.

Knowledge of the displaced environment is a bit like the once forbidden knowledge of good and evil; once we have it we cannot get rid of it. Those who have it are likely to find the behaviour of those who do not have it irrelevant and even irritating; they are anxious, like Eve, to share the fruit. As the example of artillery in the *Iliad* suggests, all of us have already tasted of it to some degree. The guide who is ignorant of what is known travels blind in territory that others can see.

3
KNOWLEDGES OF THE PAST

> Have patience. History is not yet what it ought to be. That is no reason to make history as it can be the scapegoat for the sins which belong to bad history alone.
>
> Marc Bloch

It is one thing to acknowledge that a displacement of environment inevitably occurs as time passes and that the meaning of literary works is changed as a consequence, but another to suppose that anything can be done to compensate for it. Critics are resigned to the fact that the environment of the primitive epics can only be guessed at; should they not acknowledge that similar irretrievable damage has been done to their understanding and appreciation of all past works of literature and make whatever they can of them, treating them as different from primitive epics in degree but not in kind? Our answer to this question will probably depend both on our awareness of the extent to which displacement of environment changes the meaning of a text and on our view of the possibility of recovering knowledge of the environment that has been displaced.[1]

Sceptics who dismiss the likelihood that such knowledge can be usefully recovered have to acknowledge that a modicum of it is inescapable for any experienced reader. Even a casual acquaintance with the literature of the past provides us with information about the environments in which it was written, and we learn very early to distinguish between contemporary books and books that were written before we were born. We accommodate ourselves effortlessly to the concerns and assumptions of, say, Shakespeare's plays in much the same way that we accommodate ourselves to the obsolete language in which they are conveyed. Ignoring the pastness of past works of literature is possible to conceive of but impossible to do. The choice is really between reading with a sense of the past that is derived casually and unreflectively and reading with a sense of the past that is arrived at deliberately and methodically.[2] Or, to put the matter in another way, the choice is not between reading past works in the light of the past or in the light of the present, but between reading them in the light of a very inaccurately imagined past or in the light of a less inaccurately imagined past. Neither alternative may seem very satisfactory, but one seems less unsatisfactory than the other.

I

The extent to which we can retrieve the past is a problem that has been addressed with considerable subtlety by philosophers of history. Among those opposing scepticism, one of the more fruitful recent lines of investigation into the possibility of genuine knowledge of the past has been to take a hard look at the nature of our knowledge of the present, to note its limitations, and then to compare these with the recognized limits to our knowledge of the past.[3]

Our knowledge of the present is acquired in a great variety of ways and we are often unconscious of them. For the purposes of comparing it with our knowledge of the past it is useful to distinguish three main categories of knowledge: knowledge derived from direct observation (direct knowledge); knowledge derived from indirect observation (indirect knowledge); and knowledge already possessed at the moment of direct or indirect observation (previous knowledge).[4] Previous knowledge differs in kind from direct knowledge and indirect knowledge in that it is derived from their past evidence and modifies our perception of their evidence thereafter.

Direct knowledge, knowledge derived from direct observation, is the kind that common sense has led us to rely on most. We are used to thinking that we are surer of what we can see, hear, taste, touch, or smell than we are of any other data,[5] and a large part of the energy of philosophical and religious thought over the ages has been devoted to efforts to limit or qualify that feeling of certainty by making us aware of its weaknesses. Accordingly our educations usually draw to our attention characteristic failures of the five senses. That we continue to depend upon the senses is the consequence of the vividness of their evidence, the fact that most of our earliest knowledge seems to be acquired by way of them, and the experience that they prove reliable for most day-to-day needs. It has not escaped the attention of either philosophers or theologians that knowledge derived from direct observation is the kind that we share most obviously with the rest of the animal world.[6]

Indirect knowledge, knowledge derived from indirect observation – that is, from observation by other people – is what distinguishes the well-informed person from the ignoramus. In pre-literate or illiterate societies knowledge of this kind is largely derived from the personal testimony of other people; in the civilized world, however, such testimony is enriched and made much more elaborate by being provided in documentary form. Knowledge derived from indirect observation is the essence of formal education, allowing our knowledge to outstrip our personal experience, and while it is greatly valued it is traditionally presented as needing sceptical scrutiny. We are advised not to believe everything we read. We are encouraged to form the habit of questioning reports of phenomena that conflict with our direct knowledge, but at the same time we learn not to dismiss such phenomena out of hand. Until the invention of film the knowledge that all but a tiny minority had of the appearance, conduct, and extent of the rest of the world was largely dependent on knowledge derived from indirect observation.[7] Great empires have been developed and great wars have been fought on the basis of indirect observation; indeed, almost any human activity practised on a grand scale necessitates our reliance on evidence that is supplied by the testimony of others.

Previous knowledge, the knowledge that precedes any particular observation, is more complex and elusive, but no less important than direct knowledge and indirect knowledge. It is possible to imagine a stage in infancy when direct observation is not preceded by experience and hence by expectation, but this period of life is not really accessible to us in a verifiable form. The development of the knowledge that precedes observation is part of the conscious experience of everyone. When we eat, for example, we choose food with the expectation that it will taste as it has tasted on previous occasions. Anyone who has sprinkled salt on food thinking it to be sugar will know how much greater the shock of tasting it is than when one knows in advance that one is doing so. The object that we perceive may be the same but our perception of it is modified by the knowledge that we had previous to our observation of it. In this instance the knowledge that precedes observation, previous knowledge, is itself derived from even earlier direct knowledge. Previous knowledge can also be derived from earlier indirect knowledge. Through direct knowledge the surface of the earth appears to be flat, but we learn from indirect knowledge (the testimony of others) that it is in fact curved. If our education is at all scientific we may also have had phenomena drawn to our attention (direct knowledge) that appear to confirm the curve of the earth's surface and to be incompatible with its being flat. We learn to reject our perception of the flatness (direct knowledge) in favour of the reported curvedness (indirect knowledge). Previous knowledge similarly overrides direct knowledge when we cease to think of the sun and moon being the size of large coins.

The three categories of knowledge are part of the equipment of all rational beings from their earliest years; each category is capable in certain circumstances of claiming authority over either or both of the others. It has seemed worthwhile to go over this familiar ground because the relationship of the three kinds of knowledge to one another in our knowledge of the present is different in some respects from their relationship to one another in our knowledge of the past, and the differences bear on our attitude to the recovery of the past.

Our knowledge of the present is not confined to what is happening at this very moment. We commonly extend the 'present' back into our own past experience to mean the time since we first became conscious of our surroundings and distinguish this present which has a past of its own from the 'past' that was previous to our consciousness. Our knowledge of the present in this extended sense may still be divided into the three categories of direct knowledge, indirect knowledge, and previous knowledge, but is modified by memory. Before considering the effect of memory on each of these categories it will be useful to pause for a moment to examine the way in which knowledge is transmitted or preserved by memory and to consider both how our knowledge of what we did yesterday differs from our knowledge of what we are doing now, and how our knowledge of what we did yesterday also differs from our knowledge of what we did years ago.

An essential difference between our knowledge of what we did yesterday and what we are doing now is that yesterday's experience is complete. This statement may seem too obvious to need to be made, but its consequences are so important that it deserves to be acknowledged explicitly. If, for example, one observes something happening that one does not quite understand, it is often possible to examine it more closely; if one is puzzled today by something that happened yesterday, one cannot examine it more closely. The kind of knowledge we are speaking of here is direct knowledge. All that one can do is examine one's recollection of what happened yesterday; it is essentially unimprovable as a perception once it is finished.[8]

Furthermore, as time passes, our memory of what we have ourselves experienced decays, usually to the point where we can no longer see what happened in our 'mind's eye' but remember instead what was significant about it. Our memories of things we have done or seen repeatedly (rooms we have lived in for long periods of time, for example) seem to be the most firmly entrenched in our recollection. One can ask how many chairs were in such a room and count them for the first time many years after having last seen the room by remembering one's repeated experience of the room. Unique experiences are much more difficult to remember in this way unless some special significance that is attached to them has kept them fresh in our minds. Direct knowledge is at its best at the moment of perception and decays thereafter, often being totally forgotten.

The effect of the passage of time on indirect knowledge is less severe. Knowledge acquired in this way is of course subjected to direct observation when it is acquired. One usually has a clearer sense of what one is told at the moment of being told it than one will have a day later and a much clearer sense than one will have years later. Generally our recollection of what is said degenerates from awareness of the very words spoken to an awareness of the gist of what was said. In certain respects, however, indirect knowledge resists decay in ways that direct knowledge does not. In the first place it is, by definition, shared. Someone who tells us something is likely to be able to supplement or confirm our knowledge of what it was. If the indirect observation was by way of any form of document (newspaper, book, picture, the testimony of reporters on the television news, etc.), the document that provided the knowledge may be re-examined if it has been preserved. For indirect knowledge, in other words, we need not rely on memory only and by renewing it we may even improve it and keep it fresh indefinitely.

Previous knowledge seems to decay least of all. Once we know that the surface of the earth is curved we know it for the rest of our lives. The reasons for the exemption of previous knowledge from the decay associated with memory are difficult to be sure of, but what matters here is that previous knowledge is relatively exempt.[9] Unless it is knowledge original with oneself and not shared with others it is also capable of being verified and renewed by others.

The fact that we are more reliant on memory for direct knowledge than for indirect and previous knowledge has a bearing on the relative authority we accord each category of memory. At the moment at which knowledge is acquired, direct observation is relied upon more than indirect knowledge or previous knowledge. If we look at the sky and perceive that it is blue we do not question our perception. If we look at the sky and perceive that it is yellow we may be surprised (because of previous knowledge) but we are likely to question our perception only if, for example, another observer claims that it is blue (indirect knowledge) or if, for example, we are aware that we are suffering from jaundice (previous knowledge).[10]

With the passage of time the authority of direct knowledge which is paramount at the moment of acquisition – though even then not beyond challenge – declines. We are familiar with the way in which people who have shared experiences can differ in their recollection of them. Two people who have gone on a picnic years before will argue with a third about where it was held. Recourse to a photograph album may reveal that all three are mistaken in their recollection, and yet even their combined memories of their personal experience, direct knowledge, will bow before the indirect knowledge provided by the photograph. Our willingness to forgo even the certainty of our recollection of direct knowledge arises from another use of it, our repeated observation that, while memory decays and plays us tricks, records (photographs, diaries, newspapers, etc.) do not change.

The precedence of the authority of indirect knowledge in our sense of our own past experience is not total; direct knowledge and previous knowledge are mutually corrective. It is by no means an uncommon experience to read, say, a newspaper account of an event that one has witnessed personally and to feel sure that the report is inaccurate. If one's experience of newspapers were consistently at odds with one's personal experience of events one would probably give up reading them. Most of us develop a measure of scepticism and in important matters would seek further corroboration. Here the problem is not with indirect knowledge *per se* but with a form of it that because of the conditions in which it is gathered and disseminated requires haste and encourages exaggeration. Other kinds of indirect observation – diaries, books, conscientiously prepared magazine articles – are usually more reliable, but the critical scrutiny of indirect knowledge by our memory of direct knowledge is one of the crucial distinctions between our knowledge of the past we have lived through and the past that precedes our personal experience.

The effect of the passing of time on previous knowledge differs from its effect on direct knowledge and indirect knowledge. Whereas direct knowledge deteriorates and indirect knowledge often remains very much the same, previous knowledge is capable of improving. It is possible, for example, to experience an event by direct observation and to come to understand one's experience better in the light of knowledge acquired later. The knowledge acquired later may be derived from either subsequent direct knowledge or subsequent indirect knowledge, and it belongs to the category of previous knowledge in the sense that it is active previous to the renewed consideration of the past event. An example of this phenomenon would be the direct observation of planting bulbs that failed to come up and supposing that the failure was due to the poor quality of the bulbs or of the soil or to the inclement weather. If, the following autumn, someone pointed out that one was planting one's bulbs upside-down, the failure of the previous spring would be 'known' in a quite different way from how it was known before, and better.

When we come to the past, in the sense of the period before we ourselves became conscious, only two of the three categories of knowledge seem to be possible. Direct knowledge appears to be unavailable to us either as a new direct experience – we cannot be there – or as a recollected direct experience – we cannot remember being there. This limitation is the most serious and the most obvious obstacle to our knowledge of the past, but even this is not complete. It is true that we cannot witness past events or meet people who died before we were born, but much of what made up the physical environment of the past is still extant. Some of its most evocative and significant objects are unchanged. The Atlantic Ocean that Columbus sailed across or the Alps that Hannibal climbed over may be differently perceived by passengers in modern ships or planes, but the object that is directly observed, the object of direct knowledge, remains essentially the same even if as a consequence of previous knowledge we perceive it differently. Small physical objects, artefacts as well as natural phenomena, also survive. One can hold in one's hand an ancient Roman coin and repeat the action of people who lived 2,000 years ago. Again in such instances the direct knowledge, of which no record exists, appears to be repeatable; our indirect knowledge and previous knowledge are what may have changed, although it may be possible to discover something of what they were for an ancient Roman.[11]

Indirect knowledge survives unequally from the past. From about 1800 on, the documentary evidence for it survives in such bulk in most advanced civilizations that looking for representative selections is like searching for needles in haystacks. Prior to 1800 the survival of documents is less reliable, and prior to the introduction of printing the records are so fragmentary that even if one has access to them it is difficult to be sure how typical they are. But where they exist they are invaluable indications of what the past was like just as modern ones are invaluable indications of what the present is like. Their weakness is that we often cannot set them against direct knowledge as we can their modern counterparts. This handicap which we face as students of the past can be allowed for only by being alertly sceptical of our results.

The previous knowledge of the past requires a different approach. Since previous knowledge is by its very nature cumulative, our problem is not that it is likely to have been lost but that we have more of it than our predecessors had. Even allowing for lost skills – the ability to use a sword, ride a horse, sew a fine seam, etc. – we are more likely to overlook differences between the past and our own time by attributing expectations and attitudes to our predecessors that we ourselves take for granted but that were unknown to them. In trying to understand the experience of Columbus and his crew as they sailed towards America it is presumably of considerable importance to know how sure they were that the surface of the earth was curved. The ancient Greeks had been able both to demonstrate that the earth was spherical and to calculate its circumference with considerable accuracy; was this knowledge part of the previous knowledge of Spanish sailors in the fifteenth century? Learning about the state of previous knowledge in the past is often a matter of inference and, while knowledge generally seems to advance, losses accompany the gains and there are periods such as the Dark Ages in which much of what was known by earlier generations seems to be altogether lost sight of. We rely for our information about previous knowledge in the past upon the records provided by indirect knowledge, and here too great caution is in order. Those who commit what they know to writing are usually the most elaborately informed people in a community, and until the Renaissance they were attempting to communicate mainly with other elaborately informed people. The retrieval of previous knowledge has been the special province of the history of ideas, but it is a field in which the history of information may be a necessary preparation. Provided that indirect knowledge survives, it should be possible to arrive at previous knowledge as it existed at various times in the past by following much the same process as was followed by those who received education based on indirect knowledge in the past. Our problem is not that we cannot learn what they learned but that we must develop the ability to think as if we had forgotten what has been learned since.

II

Historical criticism is so closely akin to the practice of history in its ambitions and its materials that a discussion of the nature of our knowledge of the past that serves the latter serves the former too. But because the aims of the historical critic are more limited than the aims of the historian, and because the relationship of historical criticism to its materials is different from the relationship of history to its materials, certain important distinctions need to be made.

Perhaps the most important of these differences is that, whereas the historian must be attentive to the untypical and rare in the past as well as to the ordinary and is interested in what actually happened as well as in what seemed to have happened, the historical critic wishes to know mainly what was typical and apparent. This difference arises because the historical critic is interested in the past as a means to an end, that end being to understand literary works from the past as they were understood when they were new.[12] Since the means to arriving at such an understanding is recovery of the displaced environment and the displaced environment was characterized as one shared by author and readers, the emphasis is on the typical and on the apparent even if the apparent is untrue. An author with special knowledge that was not shared by readers would have been obliged either to suppress or to explain it, or to risk failing to communicate satisfactorily. Such failures of communication have certainly occurred, but they are almost by definition exceptions to the normal way in which literary works function. This limitation of the historical critic's field of interest sharply reduces the importance of the loss of knowledge based on direct observation in the past. If the personal experience of an author is out of bounds unless it is reflected in the personal experience of readers, the loss of this recollection of direct experience (the chief loss involved in our knowledge of the past) becomes almost irrelevant to our understanding of the literature of the past. Direct experience that is shared or typical, however (the experience of being in love, of hoping, fearing, learning, ageing, and so on), repeats itself century after century in a way that makes it one of our most reliable links with our predecessors. The special handicap of the historian is much less serious for the historical critic.

A second difference between traditional historians and historical critics is one of which some modern historians are also acutely aware – that historical critics must blot from their mind as much as possible whatever may have happened after the literary work they are criticizing was published. Their sense of history as a continuum in which causes have effects and in which the effects have come to seem more or less significant is replaced by a history that has come to an end abruptly with the work in question.[13] In this respect, it should be added, historical critics also differ from literary historians, who concentrate on a progression of influences and inter-connections between literary works, in that the former wish to declare out of court all of these that would not have been part of the awareness of readers contemporary with the work. The challenge here is a variant of the challenge posed by previous knowledge in the past: historical critics must develop the ability to suppress their anachronistic previous knowledge, no matter how important they may think it at other times when they are not practising historical criticism.

Because what we know cannot be turned on and off like a tap, and because of the complexity of human consciousness, the notion of suppressing anachronistic previous knowledge is a crude approximation. An analogous problem, our state of mind when we attend a play, has vexed would-be definers for centuries. But there seems to be general agreement that we can enter imaginatively into the fictional world of a play in a way that differs from how we would witness 'real life', and that the world of the play has a consistency of its own on which we avoid intruding our everyday expectations. In the case of an old play the analogy is even closer to the aim of the historical critic; we resist the intrusion of the thought that Ophelia should have slapped Hamlet before he finished his 'Get thee to a nunnery' speech, and if it intrudes nevertheless our minds have the capacity to prevent it from interfering with our attention to the way in which she actually behaves. The suppression of anachronistic previous knowledge may be conceived of in much the same way.

The historical critic is obviously more closely aligned with the social historian than with the constitutional historian or the economic historian, but with a rather old-fashioned kind of social historian. The social historian who attempted to depict the past by relying largely on works of literature came very close indeed to the domain of the historical critic, but because it has been observed that works of literature provide evidence of the past that is not wholly reliable social history has on the whole turned towards records untainted by the demands of fiction or the rhetoric of special pleading.[14] From a historical point of view this turn seems to be justifiable, but from the point of view of the historical critic it has two drawbacks. The first is that it accentuates the emphasis on the actual rather than the apparent. If in a particular period there was a widespread perception that wandering beggars had become a serious menace to society and that perception was reflected in works of literature, it may be of historical interest to show, by systematic reference to records, that the number of wandering beggars actually diminished during the period in question; but the fact may be irrelevant to our understanding of a work written by someone who believed otherwise for readers who felt the same way. The second drawback to a retreat to the more reliable if impersonal archives of institutions, whether public or private, is that the focus of the social historian shifts away from the very aspects of social life that are most likely to be taken for granted but left unmentioned in works of literature. The bias of historical critics is just as great. To the social historian their activities and interests are likely to seem misdirected – what historical critics need most is exact and detailed information about the typical daily routine of the period of the literary work being considered, the typical equipment used, the typical circumstances, and so forth. They are less interested in evidence of undernourishment or diminished life expectancy than they are in knowing exactly what was eaten and how it was prepared. In this respect the model sought by historical critics very much resembles an unreflective modern person; they seek to become familiar with such people in the past and to come to know how they led their lives well enough to recognize departures from it.

Questions of the respective aims and biases of historians and historical critics are reflected in the different ways in which they treat their evidence. The aim of the historian may be said to be to reveal the course and nature of events in the past and to do so by examining the evidence provided by documents. The aim of the historical critic by contrast is to discover the meaning of documents in the light of past events.[15] The historian and the historical critic often use the same materials as evidence but for different ends.

The difference between a work of literature and a past event is obscured by the different sets of values assumed by literary critics and historians respectively. There is something grotesque, for example, in the realization that Richardson's *Clarissa* is arguably of as great significance to the understanding of eighteenth-century literature as the Seven Years War is to the understanding of eighteenth-century history. If we modify the comparison to one between *Clarissa* and the documents that record the events of the Seven Years War the sense of incongruity is somewhat lessened; but if we modify it further and regard *Clarissa* as a document that provides evidence of an event (Richardson's writing of *Clarissa*) it increases again. Distinctions need to be made here.

The first is the distinction between a work of literature and a historical document. A work of literature may be a historical document and a historical document may be a work of literature; the difference between them lies in the uses to which they are put. Some works of literature very rarely figure as historical documents (lyric poems, for example), and some historical documents (street directories or lists of bankruptcies, for example) are rarely if ever treated as works of literature, but these tendencies are symptomatic of the customary biases of literary critics and historians and are not intrinsic to the works of literature and historical documents. Burke's speech 'On Conciliation with the Colonies' of 1775 may serve the historian as a document that is important to an understanding of the forces that led to the American Revolution, and as a document that had an influence on people in Britain and in America who were involved in the Revolution. The speech is also of interest to the literary critic as a significant example of hortatory rhetoric. The speech is the same object for both critic and historian, but each treats it with a different end in view. For the historian a document is interesting in so far as it helps us to understand events or informs us about events; for the historical critic, events are interesting in so far as they help us to understand a particular class of document, the work of literature, a *text*. The difference between the two approaches may be expressed diagrammatically as in figure 11. Burke's speech, for example, could serve as text in both cases. Just as historians typically limit their investigations to the kinds of documents that have proved to be particularly reliable guides to events, historical critics typically limit

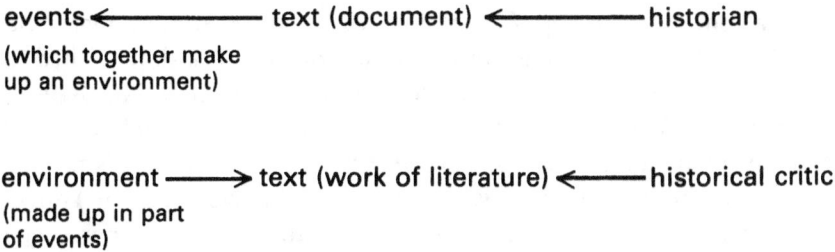

Figure 11

their investigations of events to the kind that usually have some bearing on works of literature.

While the historian and historical critic may on occasion focus their attention on the same document and, in their ways of doing so, demonstrate the difference between their respective purposes, they more commonly concentrate on topics that are quite different from one another. A typical pair might be the historian's attention to the Battle of Waterloo and the historical critic's attention to the fall of the Rebel Angels in *Paradise Lost*. In the terms we have been using, the Battle of Waterloo is an event, while *Paradise Lost* is a document or text. Historians learn about the nature of an event by examining documents that record it – Napoleon's diary, for instance. However, their interest in such documents is limited to what they tell us about the event; their interest in the event is derived from its having been seen to have had a significant relationship with other events.[16] They wish to 'know' what happened as if they had been there themselves, not merely as Napoleon or as Wellington perceived it, but as their various soldiers perceived it – in short, from various points of view. Since they cannot be present retrospectively, they must piece together documentary evidence in order to arrive at a reliable outline of what went on.

From a historian's point of view *Paradise Lost* might be used as documentary evidence of seventeenth-century political or religious attitudes but, because these would be difficult to disentangle from the requirements of the narrative, as rather suspect documentary evidence. For historical critics, however, the fall of the Rebel Angels in *Paradise Lost* is significant and interesting because of its place in the imagined world of Milton's poem. If all that survived were a summary of the poem – a collection of the 'Arguments' that precede each book, let us say – and other evidence of what the poem had been (Dryden's stage adaptation, *The State of Innocence* of 1677, for example) historical critics would have evidence of the nature of the work they wished to 'know' of very much the same kind as the evidence historians have of the Battle of Waterloo, but the evidence would cease to hold any real interest for historical critics. The difference between the historian's event and the historical critic's text is that the event can be known only by report whereas the text survives and may be experienced directly.[17] The aim of historical critics seems on the face of it much easier to achieve. Knowledge of *Paradise Lost* that was of the same quality as the historians' knowledge of the Battle of Waterloo would be useless for historical critics. What they require is more like a re-enactment of the Battle of Waterloo that can be repeated over and over again and be examined directly in various ways. However, just as historians who were able to travel in time would be astonished at how different the Battle of Waterloo seemed to be from the way in which they imagined it, historical critics who were able to observe what was imagined by one of Milton's contemporaries as he read *Paradise Lost* would presumably be astonished at the ways in which it differed from their own imaginings.

The example of a play may be helpful here in partly bridging the gulf between an event and a text. Although the texts of plays are often treated simply as works of literature that may be understood fully by being read, they are by definition part only of what constitutes a performance of a play.[18] Performance requires actors and actions, a setting for them to perform in, and so on; it not only complements the text but defines it. If we attend a performance of *Hamlet* today it will differ in many respects from any performance of *Hamlet* by Shakespeare's own company even if it is faithful to the text and makes use of all the information available to the historical critic about how the original performances were carried out. Historians of acting are familiar with the great difficulty of achieving more than the very broadest sense of how particular actors performed in the past. Inaccurate though the attempt to restage an old performance would necessarily be, its inaccuracy pales into insignificance by comparison with any attempt that might be made to restage the Battle of Waterloo. The difference arises not merely from the greater scale of the battle or from our obvious disinclination to kill or wound participants but from the enormous discrepancy between the adequacy of the text of the play on the one hand and the adequacy of the documentary evidence of the battle on the other.

Modern observers inexperienced either as historians or as historical critics would be greatly puzzled by much of what they saw if they were able to travel back in time and witness either the Battle of Waterloo or one of the original performances of *Hamlet*. It is likely that historians and historical critics would be puzzled too, although they would be less surprised by the difference between what they had expected and what they saw. A commonplace comparison would be the experience of being told what someone looked like and then meeting that person – mere recognition is the most that one could hope for, and even that frequently fails us. This inadequacy of the historical imagination or of the imagination of the historical critic should be borne in mind when we turn to texts that were meant only to be read. Historical critics may well feel that they have an advantage over historians in that the text in front of them (*Paradise Lost*, say) is the very text that was in front of Milton's contemporaries. In a sense it is as though the Battle of Waterloo could be placed before us. However, just as the text of a play requires performance, the text of a work meant only for reading requires to be imagined by the reader, to be given the equivalent of a performance in the mind. Each individual reader's imaginative performance of a text is bound to be different in various respects from the imaginative performance of other readers, and although we have very little access to those differences – they are by their very nature private and hard to share – we take them for granted. Nevertheless it seems obvious that allowing for these individual differences there are also differences between the imaginative performances of different groups of readers – between readers in different countries and between readers in different centuries. Perhaps the quickest way of gaining a sense of these differences is to look at the pictorial representations of literary works, *Paradise Lost* included, and to see how incompatible the imaginations of other periods can seem to be to our own. The problem that typically afflicts the historian is paucity of material; the historical critic by contrast is in danger of over-confidence.

III

The more limited aims of historical critics make it possible for them to abstain from the investigation of many elements of the past environment that concern historians, but also oblige them to give detailed attention to a number of matters that historians, already over-burdened, have not traditionally had time for. The most important of these is the literary environment, important because historians have for the most part, understandably, been content to derive their information about it from literary historians. The social environment matters as much to historical critics, but with it they have much more assistance from their historical colleagues. With social environment what is needed is an approach to materials that is largely the same but from a point of view that is more particularly pertinent to the understanding of works of literature.

For historical critics, the aim of the recovery of the displaced social environment is to know it as we know our own social environment. The recovery that would be ideal for the historical critic would be akin to time travel that would permit a long enough stay in a particular place for it to be possible for its features to become familiar. It would not matter very much which particular place was chosen as long as it was reasonably typical, the sort that readers of the period would have accepted unquestioningly as normal. In the absence of time travel one can hope for no more than approximations, but less satisfactory though they are they provide a kind of gain that rapidly becomes apparent by means of what may be called the principle of negative certainty.

While it is difficult to reconstitute a past scene of which one has no direct knowledge and consequently difficult to be sure how adequate any reconstitution of a past scene is, the attempt to achieve it commonly defines various alternatives that one can be sure are not accurate. These usually take the form of the imaginative modifications of our own modern circumstances that take place when we try to think about the difference between the present and the past. This experience is familiar to us all. We know, for example, that the audiences for Shakespeare's plays had no experience of internal-combustion engines, that they never travelled in aeroplanes, watched television, or spoke on the telephone. Such information, derived ultimately from historians, is so familiar to us that we are unlikely to think it particularly valuable, but the field of certainty about what was *not* part of the social environment – negative certainty – is capable of being extended gradually to include information that is not so familiar. The advantage of negative certainty is that it is useful even when it is made up of unrelated and incomplete information, the kind of information that we are most likely to acquire spontaneously about the past. But what can be acquired spontaneously can also be acquired systematically. The limits to our acquisition of negative certainties are as often the result of a failure to consider the information that is available as the result of inaccessibility of the information. The historian may well recoil from the prospect of systematic compilation of negative certainties as being unrealistically ambitious, but historical critics, dependent though they will be on the historian's skills, may actually achieve what they need because their field of interest is so much narrower and so much more closely linked to their own daily experience.

Most historical critics gain their knowledge of a displaced environment by reading widely in the literature of the period. Even by reading Shakespeare's plays anyone who is prepared to pause to look up in dictionaries and encyclopaedias whatever is unfamiliar can develop an impressive range of apposite information. But the difference between this kind of information and the knowledge we have of our own social environment will be obvious if we test it by a comparison of environments. If we take the course of an ordinary day in our lives and compare it step by step with what we know of an ordinary day in the life of, say, an Elizabethan, the deficiencies in our knowledge of the past environment are immediately revealed. Even imagining the matter of rising in the morning in a world ignorant of alarm clocks, toasters, tea, coffee, or marmalade, from a bed shared perhaps with several other people, affords potential detail of unexpected variety and is likely to increase the number of our negative certainties. Moving from negative certainties to their implications is less simple and less easy to be sure of, but the historical critic will at least wish to consider implications and to be alert for evidence that may verify or contradict them.

Negative certainties provide the quickest gains; the imaginative reconstruction of the displaced social environment is much more difficult and much more likely to involve us in gross errors. The problem here is that when we imagine the past in any detail, as, for instance, the painter of a historical scene might, we are inclined to imagine our own time with some bits of the past added. The more incomplete our knowledge of the past, the more anachronistic our best-intended imaginings are bound to be. Nevertheless, if we think about these imaginings, make a habit of submitting them to critical assessment, and allow for the probability that they fall short of what might be desired, they are likely to represent an advance over imaginings that are wholly uncoordinated.

It is, of course, possible to pursue the reconstruction of displaced social environments systematically as a social historian would; but the source materials for social history are still so incomplete that historical critics who attempt to do so will find themselves obliged to abandon criticism for history. Nevertheless, unsatisfactory though our current knowledge is, it seems likely that thinking about displaced social environments in broadly defined categories will not only increase our awareness of negative certainties but provide a rough approximation to what we are seeking. For instance, categories such as physical settings, equipment, routines, social organization, and knowledge and beliefs might be said as a group to include most of what we think of as our social environment, but the evidence for them differs greatly from category to category, and the ways in which we seek them out will necessarily differ too.

Physical settings are perhaps the most accessible. The natural surroundings are often essentially unchanged, and if historical critics live in the place in which the literature they are concerned with was written the general features of the landscape, progress of the seasons, and animal and plant life are already an important bond between them and the past environment.[19] Even with the natural environment, however, caution is needed. One should be alert to changes in landscape caused by deforestation, enclosure, the introduction of exotic plants and creatures, the effects of changes in population, the industrial revolution, and so forth. But once such changes have been assessed it is usually possible to find some locations in which typical earlier features have been preserved and to make oneself familiar with them. The physical settings of cities, towns, and villages may be expected to have changed much more, but with the exception of a handful of particular cities works of literature presuppose an awareness of the average rather than the special, and a combination of the better-preserved examples with documentary evidence provides considerable detail of what they once looked like. Even the cities most written about generally contain many features from different periods of the past, and their previous appearance is reasonably well recorded. Works such as *The Survey of London*, for example, go far towards providing a verifiable account of London back into the seventeenth century, often street by street and sometimes house by house. With public buildings that task is easier because so many survive; domestic architecture has unfortunately suffered most, and it is domestic architecture that figures most prominently in literature. It is still possible to visit and even to live in Tudor houses, however, and to reconstruct imaginatively what they were like before the introduction of plumbing, gas, or electricity.

Physical settings overlap to some extent with equipment, from the vehicles found in the streets and the paving and lighting of the streets themselves to the furnishings of rooms. Our knowledge of furniture, carpets, interior lighting and heating, etc., tends to be derived from reassembled rooms in museums; these in turn depend upon the survival of the objects themselves and upon the evidence of surviving depictions of them. It is in the nature both of the terms of survival and of the bias of most museums towards good specimens that reconstructions that use original equipment should be untypically grand. It is also typical of them that in the attempt to define a particular period they should exclude materials from an earlier period in a way that neither we nor our ancestors have excluded old chairs, tables, carpets, and so on, from our dwellings. Indeed, from the point of view of the historical critic, there is often as much to be learned from the attempts at replication of past physical settings such as Williamsburg, Virginia, in which people are employed to live in the midst of restored eighteenth-century surroundings and to carry out the daily work of people of the time with the sorts of tools they used.

The category of equipment may be thought of as embracing implements and machinery of all kinds, from needles to battering-rams, from tinder boxes to water-mills, from wheelbarrows to galleons. Information about these can be gathered gradually and vicariously by reading, but a much keener sense will be felt of how much we have to learn if it is sought methodically by comparison of environments, and even more so if the comparison involves the actual use of the commoner surviving implements. One learns more about what it felt like to ride on top of a stage-coach by riding on top of a tractor-drawn haywagon than by looking at a stage-coach in a museum. The special knowledge required to sail a galleon is not required by the historical critic (although the social historian may wish to have it), but the experience of being under sail, if possible in a large vessel, is likely to be useful.

The routines and social organization of daily life are obvious points of comparison. When did the working day begin and end in the displaced environment? How was it punctuated by pauses? How did people eat and dress and at what times? How did they keep themselves clean and warm? What sort of social contacts were they likely to have with others in the course of a day? What occupations were commonest among the reading sections of the population? To answer such questions about ourselves is easy if laborious, but as soon as we begin to answer them in detail for another environment the extent of our ignorance is immediately demonstrated. The gaps in what we know are not to be easily or quickly filled, but knowing that they are there and what sort of gaps they are can make us alert to information about them in the works of the period.

The thinking typical in past environments requires a slightly different approach. History of ideas has been allied traditionally with the history of philosophy and the history of science, the emphasis being on the turning-points of what is regarded as on the whole a progressive development from the less adequate to the more adequate. Most of what we know about thought in past environments is derived from efforts to chart this development. From the point of view of the historical critic, however, the findings of the history of ideas require considerable adaptation. Concepts such as the chain of being, primitivism, social Darwinism, and so forth, have more to do with negative certainties – before (or after) a certain period they were taken for granted – than with characterization of how people actually thought. One has only to reflect on the difficulty of defining the intellectual assumptions of our own time and on the reluctance most of us would feel at finding our thoughts generalized about to realize that such concepts are inadequate in their incompleteness and their abstractness. It may be that without a knowledge of Descartes's ideas Locke could not have written his *Essay Concerning Human Understanding*, but that the reading public contemporary with Locke had any significant knowledge of Descartes's ideas is much less likely. Again the principle of comparison of environments can be applied, but with the category of thought we must look within ourselves. Not only what we think, but what we think about, needs to be considered. We are used to publicly professed beliefs (patriotic, religious, political) differing in both their intensity and their emphasis from our own private beliefs and from what we can observe of the private beliefs of others. The same difference is likely to have existed in the social environments of the past. When Samuel Pepys congratulates himself on a period of exceptionally good health, for example, and adds, 'But am at a great loss to know whether it be my Hare's foote, or taking every morning of a pill of Turpentine, or my having left off the wearing of a gowne' (*Diary*, 31 December 1664), we are given a glimpse of thinking significantly different from our own that is not only less exalted than the thought usually addressed by the history of ideas but more detailed. To be told that people in the seventeenth century were superstitious or unscientific does not bring us nearly so close to the fabric of thought that the literature of the time must have depended on.

The aim of the recovery of the displaced literary environment may also be said to be the recovery of what was known as it was known. By comparison with the social environment, however, the literary environment is preserved with comparative completeness since the invention of printing. The special problems that have to be solved in connection with it have to do with defining its extent, examining it, and trying to understand it as it was once understood. Certain classes of literary material are known to have been ill preserved, and their library classification, 'ephemera', recognizes the fact and its explanation. They do not survive because people have not found them worth preserving. Examples include schoolbooks and children's literature, newspapers, pamphlets, cheap fiction and its predecessor the broadside ballad. Ephemera of this sort are not necessarily as important as weightier literature, but we have only to consider the part they play in our own lives to see that if one had access to them they would be an especially valuable guide to the associations and meanings that things shared for everyone in past periods.[20] The principle seems to be that the lower the level of effort that is expected on the part of the reader the more typical and reliable a work will be as a guide to the norms of literature. To say this is not to claim any merit whatsoever for ephemera on the grounds of literary value, only as the documentary evidence needed as grist to the mill of the historical critic. If some ephemera are of literary value, from an aesthetic, moral, or political point of view, that is neither here nor there for present purposes. A second principle may be hazarded in connection with ephemeral literature: that the more typical it is the less the survival of parts of it matter; an exhaustive reading of it is not likely to be much more revealing than a representative reading. Where there is cause for uneasiness is in periods such as the sixteenth century where the ephemera have largely disappeared and are known for the most part at second hand. Our ignorance of ephemera is an emphatic warning sign that a literary environment is foreign ground in which we may expect to make elementary and possibly fundamental mistakes.

The troublesome but revealing question of ephemera aside, the most obvious shortcoming in attempts to recover the literary environment is the supposition, mentioned earlier, that the works from previous periods that are highly regarded in our time must have been highly regarded in their own. Most historical critics would recognize the inadequacy of this assumption in theory, but in practice it has proved difficult to avoid. The question is one not so much of avoiding over-estimation of the 'great' authors as of deciding what to put in their place. The criteria are relatively easy to arrive at: we should concentrate our attention on works that were widely read or repeatedly read or, perhaps, briefly but intensely read (and their being widely read within a particular sector of the reading public would qualify them if one were concentrating on that sector). These are the works that other works are likely to allude to or react to and to take for granted as known. In our own time guides such as popularity charts, literary prizes, reviews, statistics concerning numbers of copies published or sold, etc., seem to provide an easy way of deciding which works can be taken for granted, but even compiling such a list of resources gives one pause. How reliable are they? Do people read the books they buy? In what ways do they read them? On what occasions? Even where information appears to be unlimited it will be a difficult and delicate task to draw reliable conclusions from it. The information from previous periods is very much less ample and it diminishes rapidly from the early nineteenth century backwards in time. It may be easier to master this information (though it has not been mastered yet by any means), but drawing conclusions from it will be proportionally more difficult.

Even if we can identify the works that were best known in their own time, there remains the problem of knowing them as they were known. Where there is external evidence, whether it be in reviews or critical essays, or in the form of adaptation, parody, or allusion, we can generally feel reasonably confident of getting the broad outlines right, but in the absence of such guides (and they are only guides) a great effort will have to be made on the basis of our grasp of the social environment to test whether the differences we have been able to discern between the period in question and our own are in fact reflected in the literary works. Such knowledge will be constituted in large measure of conjecture and it will be deplorably abstract, but it will have at least one useful if humble virtue, that of allowing us to rule out some modern assumptions as anachronistic. These literary negative certainties resemble their social counterparts, and they can often make the difference between a reading that roughly approximates the original meaning and one that is totally at odds with it.

The works that are well known in any period are not, of course, only the works that are written in the period. We are more likely at present to recognize allusions to *Othello*, *Tristram Shandy*, and *Ulysses* than to any recent book, and hardy perennials such as the Bible and the Book of Common Prayer have a steady currency that is not merely literary. With such works the hazard is not that we shall overlook them but that we shall assume that their currency with us is much the same as their currency with readers in previous periods. This hazard is especially acute with omnibus works such as the Bible, where the parts that are familiar may be shifted from time to time, but it also affects our sense of the currency of authors where we read one part of their works and our predecessors typically concentrated on another part. Further, the identification of works from the past that were current is more difficult because by its very nature reliance on them, having been taken for granted, was unmentioned and now goes unremarked. In many periods the only clue to their status is whatever evidence there may be of their having been steadily republished or of their republication having become more or less frequent.

The reading habits of previous periods are suggested in a useful way by the surviving catalogues of private libraries. Most of these have been preserved, and indeed prepared, because the libraries in question were untypically extensive, but the reappearance of certain works in catalogue after catalogue is one of the best guides we have to their past currency. An acquaintance with such books may be added to the more traditional acquaintance with books that are alluded to in the works of the period. There may be some doubt whether Sheridan expected the theatre audience of *The Rivals* to have read the books that Lydia Languish hides from her aunt in Act I – 'Quick, quick! Fling *Peregrine Pickle* under the toilette; throw *Roderick Random* into the closet; put *The Innocent Adultery* into *The Whole Duty of Man*; thrust *Lord Aimworth* under the sofa; cram *Ovid* behind the bolster; there – put *The Man of Feeling* into your pocket.' The titles alone are amusingly arranged and, like the sequence of verbs, prepositions, and names of hiding places, have a calculated verbal effect, but the historical critic will wish to know what was the status of *The Whole Duty of Man* as a book for young ladies, what work was likely to be meant by *Ovid*, and why Smollett's twenty-year-old novels are equated with novels hot off the press. This sort of information must have been common ground in 1775; to recover a sense of the displaced literary tradition requires us to acquaint ourselves not only with the books named but with their status in the minds of average readers.

IV

In trying to give some idea of what will be involved in the recovery of displaced social and literary environments it is natural to direct one's attention to the ingredients, particularly to the ingredients that have not so far been sufficiently exploited. But it will be obvious that the possession of new or better information does not of itself guarantee the recovery any more than the use of a better quality of flour guarantees the baking of a better cake. New or improved information needs to be assimilated, to be placed alongside old information or to replace outmoded information, and to become a familiar part of our imagination of the past. For the active historical critic the process of assimilation is unending and the process itself, like the process of assimilating new information about the present, is not a wholly deliberate or even wholly conscious one.

The process of historical imagination has been described in various ways by philosophers of history, just as the imagination itself has been described in various ways by poets and psychologists. The description of a state of mind, perhaps especially of a state of mind that one has directly experienced, is necessarily metaphorical; and differences of emphasis and individual preference have a way of sounding exaggerated to the point of fundamental disagreement. Many of the complications involved in describing the nature of the historical imagination are considered in R. G. Collingwood's account of history as 're-enactment of past experience' (pp. 282–302). Collingwood too concentrates on the ingredients of the historical imagination, the present objects and the inferred objects, acts, and thoughts, and on the historian's deliberate deployment of them, and he claims for re-enactment only resemblance and not identity. The analogies that occur to him are drawn from epistemology, and his awareness of the unavoidable inadequacies of re-enactment is heightened by his willingness to think of ignorance as emptiness that knowledge may impinge upon rather than as fullness that better knowledge may modify.

Historical critics, on the other hand, begin with their present experience of a past work of literature and have no temptation to fall back on notions of a *tabula rasa*.[21] Readers of *Robinson Crusoe* imagine the environment of the novel as they read. The book can be satisfying and absorbing to a child who knows nothing of the displaced environment of the early eighteenth century. An enactment is taking place here, and it is largely defined by the character of the text; the stress of the historical critic will be on the need to make the enactment a re-enactment of the enactment experienced by the early eighteenth-century reader. The historical critic's ambition is more limited than the historian's, but it is still a difficult one to define, let alone fulfil.

The example of theatrical performance is helpful here because of its shared and public nature and because it is a familiar physical embodiment of the deliberate re-enactment of the past. Anachronistic performances of say, Shakespeare's Roman plays that transfer the action from ancient Rome to Napoleonic France are commonplace on the modern stage, and many result as much from a wish to free the plays from a stultifying residue of earlier antiquarian productions as from a wish to reinterpret them. A child seeing one of these would presumably have an experience that from the point of view of historical criticism would resemble the child's experience of reading *Robinson Crusoe*. The text would have been understood in terms of the child's environment and without any awareness that an original displaced environment existed. A historical critic could take the Shakespearian performance, modify it in the light of knowledge of the displaced environment, and return it to the stage refashioned after the sort of model provided by Olivier's 1945 film of *Henry V* with its careful reconstruction of the Globe Theatre. The child seeing this performance would have an experience that came closer to a re-enactment of an Elizabethan performance than the experience gained while attending the deliberately anachronistic performance. But even so this re-enactment would still be in various ways untrue to a real Elizabethan performance, and the extent of its untruth would be impossible to ascertain. Such re-enactments have a way of coming to seem dated in turn as the passage of time reveals the presence in them of elements peculiar to the period in which they were performed; as long as the information upon which historical criticism depends improves, it will be possible to modify such performances in ways that make them truer to their original environments.

Because the results achieved by even the most accurately informed historical imagination are bound to fall short of complete accuracy, and because it seems that the level of inaccuracy can only be perceived later with the advantage of improved information, it must be acknowledged that historical critics who exercise their historical imaginations are accepting the presence in them of an element of untruth. Using the best evidence available to them, they modify their awareness of their own modern social and literary environment by adapting it to what they can learn of the displaced social and literary environment of the past work of literature they wish to understand. The effort to create an environment that constitutes a whole that may be compared to the whole we experience in our own time has obvious affinities with the aims of historical fiction, and, while historical critics may hesitate to associate their search for truth with the attempt to achieve fiction, the closeness of the parallel makes further discriminations possible.

The materials available to the writer of historical fiction, whether the writer be a Walter Scott or a Georgette Heyer, are the same as those available to the historical critic. Historical critics, like the writers of historical fiction, are vulnerable to improvements in historical knowledge, and when these improvements are made their work, in so far as it is historical, will become obsolete. Both set their sights on a historical awareness beyond that of their readers, meaning to share it with them, and if that awareness is subsequently shown to be incorrect, or if it is so persuasive that it becomes commonplace, it will cease to be of interest. However, while the materials of historical criticism and historical fiction are very much the same and while both are vulnerable to later improvements in historical knowledge (to which they may have contributed), their aims differ in certain important respects, and so, in consequence, do their ways of employing their materials.

From a historical point of view the task of writers of historical fiction is easier than the task of historical critics because the fiction for which an environment is to be imagined may be modified at the will of the writers. If there are areas of a displaced environment that they know little about they can avoid them. Historical critics begin with a text that they cannot tamper with and are challenged to provide their displaced environments. It is true that they may choose one text rather than another (if they are ill prepared in the details of, say, the legal profession, they may be wise to steer clear of plays written for the Inns of Court), but if, while they are attempting to understand their text as it was understood when it was new, they realize that it requires knowledge of an aspect of the displaced environment that they are ill equipped to explore, they will feel obliged either to remedy the deficiency in themselves or to warn their readers of it. Their aim differs from that of the writer of historical fiction most signally in that the aesthetically satisfying whole they seek is that of the texts they are trying to understand and not that of texts they are trying to create. If their historical data are inadequate they have an obligation to reveal the fact, whereas writers of historical fiction have a perfectly respectable motive for concealing it.

Since truth and fiction are traditionally regarded as opposites, it may seem less damaging to the respectability of historical criticism to present the alternatives as facts and hypotheses. The historical imagination that provides us with a displaced environment, whether in the service of historical criticism or of historical fiction, may be regarded as a hypothetical reconstruction based on some facts and potentially subject to modification and correction in the light of other facts. The fictive element here is shared with science. But unlike science, historical criticism and historical fiction cannot wait until the recovery of the displaced environment is complete, in part because it is motivated by a wish to serve the reader who is alive now and who requires the displaced environment as an imagined whole, and in part because the recovery of the displaced environment will never be complete. Furthermore, because both the historical critic and the writer of historical fiction are challenged to imagine an entire environment about which they are only partly informed, they will do so by filling in the gaps with their own environment, consciously or unconsciously. Why should we place any credence in the status of this hypothetical reconstruction of the displaced environment? The answer is that we have no alternative.

When we read a text we imagine an environment. As has been explained in the last chapter, we take for granted the environment we are used to living in unless or until some discrepancy between this and the text makes us aware of a displaced environment. The habit of reading and the residue of historical awareness that we all have, no matter how little sympathy we may have for the past or how little effort we may have made to learn something about it, supply us with a substitute for the displaced environment that helps to make up for the discrepancy observed between the text and our own environment. This minimal effort at historical imagination is unavoidable, but its quality will seem seriously deficient to any reader whose historical imagination has been deliberately cultivated. The effort of even the most cultivated historical imagination seems likely in turn to be seriously deficient as a recovery of the displaced environment, as most historical critics will readily admit. When we read a past work of literature, there will be, between our own environment and the displaced environment, various attempts to recover the displaced environment that will differ from one another in degree but not in kind. Here again the imperfect analogy of theatrical performance seems to be helpful.

Readers do not ordinarily imagine the world of their texts in the sort of detail that is typical of the theatrical presentation of a text. But directors of such an adaptation, of a novel as a film, for example, while they may omit parts of their text and alter others, are committed to bringing to life not merely what is explicitly mentioned in certain parts of the text but to dealing with the implied consequences. In Tony Richardson's 1963 film of Fielding's *Tom Jones*, for example, Mr Allworthy is seen seated in his library; some decision has to be made by the director about the books that are to appear on his shelves. The modern reader may allow this element of the scene to remain dormant (the scene might be set in the scullery for all the difference it would make) or may dimly imagine a room with old books on the shelves, but in the film they must be particular old books. If the scene is being performed in eighteenth-century costume with an attempt to recover the displaced environment of the novel it will do no good to have shelves filled with Victorian books. It is a relatively simple act of historical criticism to supply calf-bound volumes typical of the period in question (the expedient actually chosen in the film). By increasing the degree of historical awareness the historical critic may consider that, because hardcover books do not deteriorate as fast as paperbacks, those who have libraries of them usually have volumes on their shelves that may be a century or more old, and Mr Allworthy's having only books directly contemporary with him in his library suggests that he is a member of the *nouveau riche* – a suggestion borne out neither by the novel nor, in other respects, by the film. Theatrical presentation makes us publicly aware of inadequacies as historical critics that we can ignore more easily in the privacy of our reading.

But if even a carefully reconstructed film like *Tom Jones* can fall short, providing gas lanterns on purportedly eighteenth-century streets, showing a Somerset landscape prematurely enclosed by hedgerows and fences, and so on, is there any point in attempting more reconstructions that are bound to fall short? The point of doing so is that literature that is not brought to life in this way in the mind has been only half read and that the more historical imagination we can bring to bear on reading it the closer we shall come to the displaced environment and the less accidental distortion there will be in our sense of what the text meant when it was new. The inevitable lapses of the historical imagination, embarrassing though it is to become aware of them after the event, are far less damaging to our experience of past literature than is the failure to exercise it.

4

STRATEGIES

> But by far the greatest obstacle to the progress of science and to the undertaking of new tasks and provinces therein is found in this – that men despair and think things impossible.
>
> Francis Bacon

I

The implications of an argument in favour of historical criticism are not simply that more critics should be historical. Historical criticism even at its best has fallen far short of what it aspires to be, and its shortcomings have no doubt much to do with its seeming to be less necessary than it really is. What is needed is deliberate and steady access to historical criticism of a kind we have so far had rarely and by accident.

Historical criticism has been contributed to most effectively in the past by people who have been widely read in the literature and other documentary evidence of the period to which the works they are criticizing belong. Acting on the commonsense assumption that the more you know about a thing the better you will understand it, such historical critics have sought to know as much as possible. Two critical approaches have been particularly rich in contributions towards the recovery of displaced environments. One is the exhaustive examination of the literary career of a single major author; the other is the exhaustive examination of a single genre in a defined period. These approaches do not have much in common with one another, but the former comes as close to the recovery of the social environment and the latter as close to the recovery of the literary environment as any historical criticism has done hitherto. Both these kinds of criticism have been conducted by a minority, but they are familiar because other types of literary criticism have come to rely on their most eminent exemplars as fixed points to which more conjectural sallies may be attached.

The single-author approach has several advantages. The scale of the enterprise even for authors who were prolific and whose lives are amply documented – Milton, Pope, Wordsworth, Byron, Dickens, etc. – is not impossibly large for the individual scholar. Letters and diaries provide access to the social environment that is detailed if unsystematic; those of a single author have a coherent point of view of the kind that we are used to in our experience of our own environment, and because they reflect the progressive transformations imposed by the passage of time in the author's life they offer reminders of alternative perspectives. The author's published works provide access to the literary environment as it was experienced and referred to by at least one author. Furthermore, prolonged specialization in the work of a single major author, of the sort required to master all the evidence, is well known to result in the absorption of many of the author's attitudes and assumptions. This absorption is neither wholly conscious nor wholly reliable, but it is common knowledge that one can often benefit from such a critic's ability to sense incongruities and errors in one's comments on the author in question.

Single-author studies have tended for obvious reasons to revolve around major authors. From the point of view of historical criticism, however, it will be apparent that more is to be learned about the social environment from the life of, say, Boswell, than from the life of Shakespeare. When the social environment is the object of the exercise, ample life records matter more than literary eminence, and it may be that study of diarists like Joseph Farington or Crabb Robinson will ultimately prove more useful to the cause of historical criticism than will study of the literary giants whose opinions they sedulously recorded.

The detail involved in single-author scholarship can be very considerable. The case of Samuel Taylor Coleridge is reasonably representative of a number of authors who have undergone major re-editing in the past thirty or forty years. His writings – including letters, notebooks, journalism, poetry, and formal prose – will amount to about forty volumes by the time the editions now under way are completed, and the manuscript remains that lie behind them constitute perhaps a third or even a half of that amount. Specialists in Coleridge typically read his writings over and over, rather as one sweeps a minefield, beginning again at the beginning each time they come to the end. As their recollection of this mass of material improves, they are likely to branch out into similar readings – not usually repeated because of the time involved – of the writings of Coleridge's circle, of Robert Southey, Francis Wrangham, and George Dyer, as well as of the more widely known Charles Lamb, Wordsworth, and Walter Scott, all of which are approached from a perspective defined by its Coleridgean focus. The particulars of Coleridge's life stimulate curiosity about the circumstances in which it was lived. The places he stayed in for prolonged periods – great cities such as London and Rome; significant towns such as Cambridge, Bristol, Keswick, Göttingen, and Valletta; villages such as Ottery St Mary, Nether Stowey, and Highgate – may all be studied, even visited, in the hope of making his life more specifically imaginable. His intellectual development may be traced through his formal education at Christ's Hospital and Jesus College, and on through his informal contact with Thomas Beddoes and Humphry Davy in Bristol, his encounter with German thought in Göttingen, and through his massive and various reading thereafter. His ill health and opium addiction invite the student to explore the medical literature of the period, often following Coleridge's own reading of it; his recurrent financial difficulties interest one in the details of domestic and national economy. It is as though successive circular ripples were being spread out through the displaced social environment by the prolonged attention to a single author in the middle of it.

The literary environment too is likely to be scrutinized usefully because most authors are avid readers. Our modern expectations are challenged as soon as we begin to read what our author is known to have read. In the case of many authors, and certainly in the case of Coleridge, the task can be overwhelming, but even if it is pursued selectively one is brought into contact with forgotten books and often with familiar books that turn out to have been read in unfamiliar ways. Access to the literary environment is likely to be less usefully representative than access to the social environment because authors are more likely to resemble their contemporaries in their experience of life in general than in their experience of literature.

The shortcomings of single-author scholarship when it is applied to criticism in general are familiar. Literary works are looked upon as illustrations of a literary life; works by rival authors are treated grudgingly or even with hostility; the author's works, appreciated one by one by his contemporaries, are regarded as a related whole, foreshadowing or echoing one another.[1] Not all single-author critics err in these ways, but single-author criticism makes such errors difficult to avoid. It also encourages the critic to consider works from an authorial point of view which unless it was available to the author's contemporaries may be perfectly valid as an element in the examination of an author's manner of composition but is irrelevant to historical criticism – that is, to understanding works as they were understood when they were new. It may be added that single-author critics rarely make all the use of their knowledge that, as historical critics, they might. Although they almost always observe many respects in which their author's life and outlook differ from what general studies of the period have led them to expect, their tendency is to attribute such discrepancies to the exceptional character of their author without pursuing the possibility that what they are observing is the difference between an actual person and a widely received but inaccurate abstraction.

The exhaustive study of a genre during a limited period of time has proved to be another major and effective aid to historical criticism, bearing particularly on the recovery of the displaced literary environment. Its most successful deployment in English criticism has been in the field of Renaissance drama. The original motivation for it seems to have been similar to the original motivation for single-author specialization, the wish to understand the works of a particular author, in this case Shakespeare, more fully. But the lack of evidence of Shakespeare's life and of the lives of his theatrical contemporaries made this approach relatively unprofitable, and comparison of his plays with those by his contemporaries seemed more promising. Just as accidents of history deprived investigators of evidence of Shakespeare the man, accidents of history provided considerable evidence of his theatre. For a start, because playgoing involved public assembly it was regulated by law. Before plays could be performed in London they had to be submitted for licensing to the office of the Lord Chamberlain and when they were published their titles were entered in the Stationers' Register. It was possible, therefore, to compile relatively complete lists of the plays performed during Shakespeare's career and to locate surviving copies of ones that were published.[2] Hardly any manuscript copies are known. Gradually all the information that survived has been identified, recorded, and analysed. The lists of plays culminated in W.W. Greg's *A Bibliography of the English Printed Drama* (1939–59). Companion studies of the acting companies and the theatres in which they performed were prepared by E.K. Chambers – *The Elizabethan Stage* (1923) – and G.E. Bentley

– *The Jacobean and Caroline Stage* (1941–68). These great enterprises, within the capacity of only the most resolute and indefatigable scholars to complete, would have been impossible had evidence survived on the scale that one associates with, say, the nineteenth century. We may feel reasonably confident that almost all the surviving evidence of the sixteenth- and seventeenth-century theatre has now been identified and assembled, but at the same time we are aware that there is much left unknown. Even the shape and size of Shakespeare's stage remains a matter of controversy.

The same desire to know all that one could about Shakespeare influenced the examination of the texts of his plays. Lacking manuscripts and being uncertain even about what manuscripts of plays in the period would have looked like, scholars have scrutinized the published versions with increasing exactness. The end results have been editions of various Renaissance dramas of great textual scrupulosity, compilations such as Charlton Hinman's *First Folio of Shakespeare* (1968) and that ingenious instrument the Hinman collator, a machine that made swift letter by letter comparison of variant copies of any Renaissance edition possible. Work of this kind is still undergoing further refinement and, championed by apologists such as Fredson Bowers, has been adapted to more modern periods and applied to other genres in circumstances that are by no means so destitute of alternative resources for establishing texts as are the late sixteenth and early seventeenth centuries.[3]

The effect on studies of Renaissance drama, however, seems to have been largely beneficial. The interest in texts as an academic exercise has made editions of many plays by minor dramatists available, and has made us aware of the machinery of publication as never before. The entire English printed drama of the period has been republished in microfiche form, and critical studies of slices of this material – revenge tragedy, citizen comedy, etc. – have provided us with a livelier and more complete sense of the theatrical literary environment of this period than we have of any other and have made a familiar acquaintance with that environment one of the requirements expected of its critics.

While single-genre criticism has done much to reveal and define the possibilities open to historical criticism, like single-author specialization it has certain limitations that from the point of view of historical criticism can come ultimately to seem like impediments.

One of these is the tendency to extend the field not by adding other genres but by moving into other periods. In the case of Renaissance drama the expansion into drama as a whole is so familiar in academic circles as to seem inevitable and indeed from many points of view desirable. From the limited perspective of historical criticism, however, the effect of pursuing a genre into other periods is to lessen the accidental side-effect of awareness of a particular displaced literary environment. A critic who has read, say, 500 plays contemporary with Shakespeare is in a far better position to appreciate the niceties of the literary environment referred to in *Othello* than a critic who has read 500 plays spread representatively over western drama from ancient Greece to the present. The temptation to expand into other periods because of their intrinsic interest and because of the ways in which they modify our understanding of drama as a genre is reinforced for the specialist in Renaissance drama by the difficulty of carrying the traditional work further. The rewards of exhaustive study of the single genre in its limited period have begun to diminish, but the circumstances that made the topic so inviting in the first place are unusual if not unique. The motive that lay behind the exhaustive approach to Renaissance drama lies behind no other genre in the Renaissance; the limitation of evidence and the public nature of much of it are not to be found in later periods.

What the historical critic will wish for is an extension of the study of the theatrical aspect of the literary environment into all the other aspects of the literary environment. Indeed, had the study of Renaissance drama been carried out with the aims of historical criticism in mind the inadequacies of an approach that left unexamined other contemporary forms of literature as obscure as many of the plays would have been obvious from the start. But the cause of historical criticism has only been served as a by-product.

Both single-author specialization and single-genre specialization have depended on the existence of arbitrary limits intrinsic to the field of study. Within the stipulated limits each aims to take into account all the evidence available. Typically the fields of study, even though limited, are very large, and if they were not they would be of less profit to the historical critic; what limits them is the intellectual energy and the length of career of the individual scholar. To observe that a lifetime can be absorbed by the study of Milton or by the study of Renaissance drama is to acknowledge that scholars are mortal. However, although we may be resigned to the view that while life is short art is long, it is not clear that the study of literature is art in quite the sense usually meant.

Here one comes to one of those troublesome conflicts that seem to require a choice between two alternatives that we are accustomed to value. One is the advance of human knowledge and the other is the well-rounded development of our individual minds. In the sciences this choice was made long ago and although many scientists exemplify the well-rounded mind they do not as a rule link it directly to the quality of their scientific activity. The distress that the student of literature is likely to feel at the prospect of an exhaustive reading of a corpus of penny dreadfuls or comic books does not find a counterpart in the scientist who considers carrying out an exhaustive series of experiments on the genetic characteristics of a fruit fly. For the scientist the two requirements are the feasibility of the experiments and the potential usefulness of the results; the moral or aesthetic considerations (shall I be a better person for doing this? shall I find the work interesting or pleasing in itself, quite apart from its conclusions?) do not arise.

In several respects modern literary criticism resembles science before the scientific revolution. Its fields are vaguely and accidentally defined; the work of its various practitioners is uncoordinated and has no agreed-upon goals. It is frequently incapable of progression. Even modern science is not wholly 'scientific' in these senses, but the contrast between it and literary criticism is not merely the one vulgarly acknowledged between scientific certainties and humanistic probabilities. Subjects such as truth and beauty are resistant to progress and seem to defy the search for certainties, but subjects such as displaced social and literary environments are not limited in the same way. We may disagree about the value of life and literature in the seventeenth century, but we should be able to agree about what evidence of its nature is available to us. In the past, historical criticism has benefited from studies that in order to make their case needed such information and sought it deliberately and methodically. The relationship of historical criticism to such work has been somewhat like the relationship of the gardener to the botanist. Gardeners, like most literary critics, prefer some plants to others. They declare war on a whole class of plants that are denominated as weeds and concentrate their attention on a handful of agreed-on favourites (the tulip, the rose, the chrysanthemum). They may become exceedingly knowledgeable about particular plants, specializing in their nurture, or they may concentrate on achieving a pleasing appearance of the garden as a whole. But when their favourite plants are afflicted with a blight, when their lawns grow thin or their vines wither, they are apt to seek botanical advice in books or from botanists of their acquaintance. Many gardeners are more knowledgeable about particular plants than most botanists are; what they usually lack is the systematic knowledge of the conditions of growth, the classes of plants, and so forth. Literary critics, historical critics included, are like gardeners, enjoying beauty, at their best presenting it skilfully for the enjoyment and enlightenment of others, but they lack a botany to fall back on in times of need. Historical critics require information about displaced environments but find that what is available to them is restricted either to a small number of subjects that have been surveyed by previous investigators for quite different purposes or to the imperfect gleanings of their own lifetimes of reading literature of the period in question. We are already indebted to others for most of what we know about the displaced environments, and it seems time to face the need to map out the range of the information we require (in the classificatory spirit of a Linnaeus, perhaps), to assign responsibility for the investigation of its various parts, and to prepare for a critical and sceptical assessment of the results.[4]

Co-operative research organized by previous agreement in order to achieve definable ends came into its own with Diderot's *Encyclopédie* and with the efforts of the French Academy to produce an authoritative dictionary. The early resistance of the English-speaking world to these developments may be put down to an innate distaste for centralization and authority or to simple jealousy, but with the great achievements of the *Encyclopaedia Britannica*, the *Oxford English Dictionary*, and the *Dictionary of National Biography*, all difficult even to imagine in, say, the 1660s, when the Royal Society was founded, that resistance may be said to have subsided. In its place is habit rather than principle. What we are used to doing one by one, and proud of doing well, we shrink from having done by teams of contributors under direction. In English studies, however, modern scholarship would be almost unthinkable without such co-operative compilations as *The Cambridge Bibliography of English Literature*, *The New Cambridge Bibliography of English Literature*, and the annual bibliographies of *PMLA*. We have come to take them for granted in somewhat the same spirit as we have come to take our encyclopaedias and dictionaries for granted. When we look for ways in which our recovery of displaced social and literary environments might be made more effective, co-operative scholarship in certain fields seems to be particularly promising. It should be seen not as a replacement for the learning of talented and assiduous individuals but as an aid to them that will probably come to seem as indispensable in the future as the reference books we take for granted today.[5]

Faith in co-operative scholarship is neither new nor particularly original, but its application to the special needs of historical criticism has been slower than one might have expected, perhaps because historical critics have characteristically been individualists and often, through their commitment to imagine the thoughts and feelings of previous generations, conservatives suspicious of the innovations of their own contemporaries. Further, technical changes of the past twenty years have vastly improved and transformed the conditions under which they work.

Most advances in historical criticism have depended on access to a broad range of information that had previously been disregarded. Such access was available in only a handful of libraries whose collections were so large and so unpremeditated in their formation as to contain even what was thought to be ephemeral or obsolete. The British Library, the Bodleian, and the Widener Library at Harvard are typical of the institutions to which historical critics have traditionally made pilgrimages and around which a fortunate few have settled permanently. Such libraries' collections take centuries to acquire. The bulk of scholarly and critical activity at universities is carried on in circumstances that are much more restricted, and limited in ways that discourage the systematic investigation of fields that have not been investigated in the past. There is no quick way of building up comprehensive libraries, but with the enormous improvements in photo-duplication it has become possible to envisage a substitute of sorts that from the point of view of the historical critic is almost as good. Microfiche series have been issued that provide all the known texts published in the English-speaking world from 1485 to 1700 and all the plays known to have been printed in English up to 1800. Runs of many periodicals that are difficult to obtain, and in some instances that do not exist complete in any single location, have been made available on microfilm. Such collections are just the beginning of a vast increase of available information, and, because they can be more complete than any single library's collection and can be worked through more methodically, they are in several respects an improvement on even the resident scholar's experience.[6] The ideal will be to produce microform versions of all texts known to have been published and to make them available in all research libraries. This happy state of affairs is a long way off, but as a concept such a resource may be considered critically, and the obstacles to it seem to be related to time, cost, and the will of its potential users.

The other revolution in the conditions of historical criticism is in the field of communications. Co-operation between scholars was hampered in the past by the need to communicate by letter and by the difficulty of providing multiple copies of one's work, especially of work as voluminous as archival research tends to be. Xeroxing has solved the problem of multiple copies, and telephone contact has made consultation swift and effective. Improvements in the speed of travel have made it possible to hold conferences of scholars involved in co-operative enterprises, allowing for an exchange of expertise while projects are at a formative stage, inviting criticism from those not personally involved, and drawing the project to the attention of potential contributors whose special knowledge may not have been identified before. These conveniences of modern life are familiar enough, but their special applicability to work on the recovery of displaced environments makes it possible to consider procedures that twenty years ago would have been impracticable.

II

It will be obvious that from the point of view of efforts to recover displaced environments some kinds of evidence survive better than others. An initial distinction may be made between what was once directly observable by the five senses and what people were once aware of by inference or by report. The objects upon which the five senses operate vary greatly in the ways in which they survive. Objects that could be seen and touched are most readily recoverable because they could be depicted or preserved. Sounds, tastes, and smells are very much more elusive and even when we think we can reconstruct them in our minds, usually by analogy with modern counterparts, it is rarely possible to verify our reconstructions.

Evidence of what people were once aware of by inference or

report, too, survives unequally. We have only to consider our own individual thoughts and feelings to realize how difficult it would be to share them as a whole with a visitor from another time and to realize that our communications of such matters are usually restricted to those few aspects in which we think our thoughts and feelings are sufficiently different from the ones usual to our community to be worth sharing or discussing. What we know is accessible also in the books from which we have learnt it, in so far as what we know is bookish in origin, and even then it has a way of losing its first freshness and precision; what we believe is often set down formally for us, in constitutions and religious manuals and the like, but our actual beliefs are often remote from these in detail and proportion, even when they are capable of being reconciled in their fundamental principles; our feelings rarely achieve official expression, but sometimes we acknowledge their presence in plays or novels or public addresses and indicate our recognition by expressing our approval in some public way.

The survival of objects that can be seen or touched seems to be the most promising field for new initiatives and is probably the best one with which to make a beginning. From the late medieval period to the present, pictorial representations of the physical social environment of our predecessors are abundant. Allowing for the 'distortions' caused by stylized representation of objects and for the unrepresentative selection of objects to which the artists' different purposes may lead, there is much to be learned about previous social environments from the careful scrutiny of their art. Hogarth's scenes, in both their painted and their engraved forms, were among the first to be used in this way and in a spirit that seems in tune with the aims of historical criticism. Realizing that the moral narratives represented by Hogarth were becoming obscure a generation or so later, the German scientist and satirist Lichtenberg published a detailed commentary on them from 1784 to 1796 which is still of use to modern viewers.[7] Lichtenberg's example, suggestive though it is, is too specific in its methods to be generally applied, but it is pertinent to any consideration of the use of art as evidence of a social environment because of its awareness of the need for historical imagination. Lichtenberg relies on his own familiarity with the environment of Hogarth's contemporaries in England, and being a foreigner he was more likely to remark upon the ordinary.[8] He wrote soon enough to be able to ask actual contemporaries of Hogarth about the nature of any puzzling elements in the environment he was trying to explain. Once the resource of personal reminiscence with its unequalled capacity for directed recollection is lost, however, quite different procedures have to be followed.

Traditionally, historical critics have used pictures as a valuable adjunct to written evidence of past periods and have gratefully pored over the splendid compilations of art historians in search of scenes that contain realistic detail of the social environment. The habit of looking at pictures in this way (which is not the way in which they were meant to be looked at and which may well seem reprehensible to the critic of art in that it reduces works of art to the level of documentary material rather as an old-fashioned social historian might have reduced works of literature) helps us to distinguish between the milieu of one century and another. While art historians, like literary critics, are more interested in what they think is first-rate art than in the mediocre and reproductions in art books reflect their bias, there is no direct connection between first-rateness in art and the faithful depiction of the physical environment – indeed, in recent times there sometimes seems to be an inverse ratio. As a consequence the pictures most readily available to historical critics are unlikely to be the ones most useful to them.[9]

Until recently there have been various obstacles to rectifying this state of affairs. The most obvious one is expense. If art books are to do justice to the pictures they reproduce – and that is the main reason for producing them – they are going to be costly. For the historical critic, however, excellence of quality (exactness of colouring, for example) is much less important, and in most cases 35 mm slides would suffice. What is required is access to a wide and representative range of examples – indeed, so far as possible, access to *all* examples. Curiously enough the most promising precedents for this sort of resource have been furnished by historians of medieval and Renaissance art who have been interested in the symbolic connotations of physical objects in pictures and who set about cataloguing them and maintaining sets of reproductions – often simple black and white photographs – to which the catalogue would lead.[10] It gradually became possible to look for the examples of, say, foxes, in medieval art and to gain a more sophisticated sense of what the presence of a fox in a particular picture might mean; historical critics made use of this resource early on in their consideration of the role of the fox in Chaucer's 'Nun's Priest's Tale', for example. But a method that can be used to collect examples of foxes can be used to collect examples of any or all physical objects, whether they be curious and unusual (such as mousetraps) or obvious and ordinary (such as shoes).

The needs of the historical critic differ in some respects from the needs of the pioneers of these reference systems for art history, but are not incompatible with capacities of the systems themselves. In the first place the goodness or badness of the art needs to be ignored. This difference is less important in the medieval period, where 'meaning' is crucial to art historians as well, but it is likely to be a dividing factor in the collection of work produced after the Renaissance – historical critics are likely at first to find their most sympathetic allies among art historians in the earlier periods. A second difference of emphasis is that the historical critic will wish to have access to every object of which a depiction survives, and not only to a wide range of examples of objects that seem to be significant to pictures. The initial catalogue will be more detailed as a consequence and will probably have to be drawn up initially not as a result of an examination of pictures but as a result of reflection on the objects that surround us today and on their counterparts in the past. To the question 'Did they use shoelaces?' it should be possible to get an exact and detailed answer from such a catalogue. The third difference is that again the historical critic is more interested in a slice of the past than in the past as part of a continuum. It should be possible to seek information about specific periods of time, 1620 to 1640, for instance, and to have it separated from evidence immediately after and (although this matters much less) from evidence immediately before.

What is needed, in effect, is a social inventory of all objects that have been depicted. These should be classified according to their use (clothing, utensils, furniture, vehicles, etc.), their date, and their place. If it is possible to distinguish between social settings on the basis of the social class or social function of the people who lived in them that classification too will be useful. Given such a resource, beyond the capacity of any individual to achieve because of its enormous scale but not unduly demanding to contribute to, requiring care and hard work rather than unusual analytical gifts or sensitivity, one might begin to be able to answer the sorts of question raised earlier concerning the activities of Dickens's Mr Dick. The essential point is that trying to look up the background of an object when a problem occurs to one is like going to the beach to match a particular shell. The odds against success are so high that the trip scarcely seems worth the effort. In the case of shells the conchologists of the nineteenth century have made the trip unnecessary by writing comprehensive catalogues; the effectiveness of the historical critic would be transformed by such a resource.

The second line of approach should be towards systematic collection of the surviving objects themselves. Such collections are useful because the weight and feel of objects tells one much about them that cannot be ascertained from pictures and, indeed, can sometimes reveal what they were used for. The difficulties that make such collections different from a social inventory of pictures are that one must have the object itself (not, as in the case of the picture, a readily reproducible image of it), that the objects have survived more imperfectly (damaged, worn out, or not at all), and that they occupy more space than the museums where they are housed can afford them. Nevertheless much could be done to make the accidental survival of objects from the past systematically useful to the historical critic.

The needs of the historical critic overlap to some extent with the aims of museums, and it is in large part the resources exhibited in museums that have kept us alive to the value of objects from displaced environments for any attempt to recover the environments. The differences between the aims of the conventional museum and the needs of the historical critic, however, are more worth pausing over because they point to possibilities that museums have, for perfectly sensible reasons, tended to avoid. As museums have developed from the cabinets of curios collected by virtuosi in the seventeenth century, the private and sometimes scientific spirit that the early collectors shared has been diverted increasingly to the public display of coveted objects that will attract visitors and, in the best museums, instruct them.[11] Splendid and costly objects (the crown jewels) or uniquely significant objects (the Rosetta stone) are the centrepieces of most museums, drawing crowds and causing problems of security. Such objects are almost by definition uninteresting to the historical critic. They are untypical of their period and they are in any case part of our common general knowledge, parts of the past environment that have not been displaced. They are expensive to acquire, expensive to maintain, expensive to exhibit, and expensive to guard.

Large collections of 'insignificant' objects, by contrast, could be accommodated in a small space, could be acquired relatively cheaply, and would offer little incentive to steal. Such museums exist, happily, but usually for narrowly defined fields. The Wellcome Museum for the History of Medical Science, for example,[12] while it makes a very serious effort to inform and educate casual visitors about medical history by means of public displays of selected objects, uses the sorts of objects that the historical critic is often denied by more conventional museums and also provides systematic access by means of catalogues to other objects that are not normally displayed. The problem of space will arise necessarily when large objects (beds, carriages, barges, etc.) are in question, but if public display is not required the space needed becomes very much less. Further, if the purpose of such a collection is not to serve the general public but rather to accommodate the serious student, the necessity of having the buildings in the expensive heart of a great city disappears, and suburban or even rural sites can be considered. All over the English-speaking world specialized museums have sprung up over the past century and a half; a co-ordinated collection of even their duplicate holdings would provide a huge resource for students, one that would allow social historians as well as historical critics to go to a single centre for study just as at present they go to a few major libraries. In addition to establishing a central collection, however, a comprehensive catalogue of all the objects held by such museums with photographs of the individual objects could be prepared – a social inventory of surviving objects to supplement the social inventory of pictures – and be made available on film at many centres to the advantage of museum curators, social historians, and historical critics alike. Such a catalogue would have the incidental but considerable advantage of bringing to light further objects hitherto neglected by a public unaware of scholarly interest in them.

Recovery of the thoughts and feelings of displaced environments followed upon the rather belated realization, not widespread until well into the eighteenth century, that the thoughts and feelings of one age can differ substantially from those of another. The earliest methodical attempts to examine the changes involved stressed their place in a continuum and attended to the thoughts and feelings that had some significant relationship to modern ones. According to Don Cameron Allen, the declared purpose of the History of Ideas Club at Johns Hopkins University, one of the most effective promoters of the subject, was 'the historical study of the development and influence of general philosophical conceptions, ethical ideas, and aesthetic fashions, in occidental literature, and of the relations of these to manifestations of the same ideas and tendencies in the history of philosophy, of science, and of political and social movements' (p. vii). To aims like these historical criticism owes most of what it knows about the different thoughts and feelings of the past. In three respects, however, what the history of ideas has aimed at in the past is not quite what historical criticism needs now. First, from the point of view of the social environment to which literary works refer, thoughts and feelings that are so complex, difficult, or novel as to tax the minds of an intellectual elite are likely to be out of bounds for writers. Second, the importance to us of an idea or a feeling has no necessary connection with its importance to people in earlier periods, and to map out previous thought and feeling with a view to showing how they turned into ours, a teleological approach, is to run the risk of overlooking altogether what once mattered most. The third weakness of the traditional history of ideas approach is that it tends to focus on change and development, the aspect of which those who are doing the thinking and feeling are generally least aware and one to which they are rarely sympathetic. Given the great service done for historical criticism by the history of ideas hitherto, are there ways in which its insights and methods can be adapted deliberately to make them even more useful to the historical critic?

One assumption that has usually been made in the history of ideas is that the present should be regarded as a norm. Although this assumption has the inconvenience of giving the history of ideas a history of its own as that norm gradually changes, it seems unavoidable because it is so much more economical than reconstructing an entire intellectual or emotional world. Acting upon this assumption, A.O. Lovejoy and others observed a number of recurrent and apparently widespread concepts in the past that were noticeable because they differed from modern concepts, and they traced their development in technical and popular literature. Concepts such as the great chain of being, primitivism (both hard and soft), romanticism, deism, and so on, were identified and described in convincing detail, to be followed, as history continued to be made, with social Darwinism, and so on.

These terms have been incorporated into historical criticism with a clarity and emphasis that might have bewildered the ages to which they have been attributed. As they have become familiar to literary critics, instances of them have been noted in popular literature and the ideas have become even more vivid because of the force of example. We may acknowledge general acquaintance with Freud's concept of the Oedipus complex in the twentieth century, but one can imagine our resistance to having it foisted on us by our successors as one of the dominating ideas of our time and exemplified by the many literary works that have mentioned it or applied it. The norm of the present is in fact most useful when it is applied generally to considering our relationship to contemporary ideas and feelings. Two principles emerge for those who are trying to recover displaced social environments: first, a considerable time elapses between the articulation of a theory and its appearance as a commonplace assumption among the reading public; second, an idea sufficiently profound or complex to be attended to by thinkers as new will be reduced to a mere caricature of itself, vulgarized almost beyond recognition, before it becomes common property. A third principle may be derived from the first, that it will be exceedingly difficult to date the different stages in the development of an idea, and the historical critic's need to separate a displaced social environment from its irrelevant future will be especially hard to satisfy.

A different but related approach to the thoughts and feelings of past periods has been exemplified in France by the founders of what has come to be known as the *Annales* school of history.[13] Historians such as Marc Bloch, Lucien Febvre, and Fernand Braudel, who have tried to enlarge the aims of history to the point where past societies could be considered as a whole, have been particularly effective in helping their readers to understand what it must have felt like to live in other periods. They too have begun with the present as a norm, and with exceptional knowledge of the physical conditions of life in the past have tried to imagine how they themselves would have felt under such circumstances.[14] The procedure has a certain kinship with 'method acting',[15] although, unlike actors, the best of the *annalistes* are so elaborately informed about their periods of specialization that they are likely to avoid gross anachronisms. From the point of view of historical criticism the greatest contribution of this kind of social history lies not so much in the detail of its particular reconstructions as in the way in which a whole alien outlook is presented dramatically and attached logically to circumstances that may be said to determine it. What the *annalistes* offer is neither wholly trustworthy nor verifiable, being arrived at on the basis of long experience animated by impressionism; but it hints at least at the way in which historical critics would like to know displaced social environments and provides an idealized sketch of the result they seek. (The single-author specialist is probably the closest literary counterpart to such historians.) While they take into account the philosophy, theology, and science of each period, they concern themselves with thoughts and feelings too simple or merely too obviously true to require to be mentioned let alone discussed at the time. Like the sounds and scents and flavours of the past, undeclared thoughts and feelings seem to be lost beyond recall, but some cautious progress can be made in their direction by re-enacting the conditions of the past or by making ourselves familiar with modern analogies to them.

III

The recovery of displaced literary environments poses a quite different group of problems from that associated with the recovery of displaced social environments, although, once again, the co-ordinated and co-operative work of many people seems to offer the most promising opportunities for advances beyond our current knowledge. If the aim of the recovery is to know a past literary environment as it was known in its own time so that reference to it in particular works will be comprehensible, three aspects will need to be considered: the range of works that existed; the portion of that range that was well enough known for authors to be able to take it for granted; and the way in which that portion was understood, in so far as it differs from the way in which a modern reader might be expected to understand it. Unlike most of the objects that existed in the past, books have a remarkably high rate of survival, at least since the invention of movable type; they have traditionally been treated as objects of value, they have been kept on shelves in a rational order that makes systematic collection of them much easier, and substantial numbers of identical copies have been manufactured.[16] The regrettable and important loss of ephemera aside (for which see pp. 83–4 above), the publication of books since the Renaissance is largely intact, even if some specific editions are not to be found.

The extent of a past literary environment is the first aspect to be considered. Traditionally there have been two ways of defining it. One is to catalogue the works of known authors and to combine the lists. Another is to examine the records of publication – the Stationers' Register, publishers' advertisements, and so on.[17] By putting together as many of these as can be found and arranging them by date of publication one can arrive at chronologically defined lists. A third method is to go through the catalogues of major libraries and to combine their holdings in order to arrive at a rough idea of what was available in a particular period.

Because the historical critic's aims differ somewhat from the aims of literary critics or general readers, the traditional methods of cataloguing do not serve historical criticism as well as they might. Almost all catalogues of libraries are arranged by author, responding to the way in which modern readers usually approach the books. In a small library this arrangement is not much of a hindrance, but in a large one, especially in one large enough to have most of the books published in any period, there is an almost irresistible physical preponderance of authors who are well known now. This modern perspective, reinforced by the existence of numerous modern editions or reprints and by the fact that the catalogues of the largest libraries are generally the creations of the past century or less, is exactly what historical critics want to avoid; what is an acknowledged convenience to the reading public poses something of an obstacle to them.

The most obvious alternatives to cataloguing libraries by the names of the authors of the books are to catalogue them by their titles, by their subject matter, or by their dates of publication. In the past one alternative has tended to preclude another, but the shift towards relatively inexpensive microfiche catalogues has made it possible to catalogue in several ways at once, or at least to provide the means of arriving at alternative kinds of catalogue relatively cheaply. From the point of view of the historical critic a catalogue arranged by date of publication is the most desirable, offering as it does the opportunity for a survey of all the works published between one date and another free of any intrusion of the preferences of later periods.[18]

One such catalogue has recently been made available by the British Library as part of its contribution to an eighteenth-century short-title catalogue. Short-title catalogues have been perhaps the most significant addition to the equipment of historical critics in the past two generations, but like libraries they are traditionally arranged by author, not by date. The British Library's publication in microfiche form of a catalogue of its eighteenth-century holdings, however, is accompanied by an index of abbreviated author and title entries arranged by year of publication.[19] One can look at all the entries for, say, 1725 and for the first time get a sense of what was actually made available to readers then. Because the British Library's holdings are very extensive such a list is already likely to be reasonably representative. Modern technology has made it possible for libraries to combine their catalogues into union lists much more easily than in the past, and work is under way towards integrating the holdings of all the major institutional and national libraries in the English-speaking world at least in a single list, in which, one hopes, it will be possible to examine the holdings by date of publication.[20]

The new eighteenth-century short-title catalogue was conceived of as a further extension of the original Pollard and Redgrave *Short-Title Catalogue* of 1946 and of its sequel by Donald Wing, and like them it takes the arrangement by author to be the most practical; but because of the greater flexibility provided by computers it has made possible a kind of access to such lists that is potentially free of the bias of modern expectations. It would be very useful to the historical critic to have the same flexibility conferred on the earlier lists by entering them too into a computer. While ways of adapting the earlier lists can be found fairly easily, the period after 1800 poses difficulties of scale. It may be that for the foreseeable future we shall have to make do with union lists of library holdings, but if these are prepared by computer it should be possible to have indexes included that are arranged by date. In conception at least there is no obstacle to having complete annals of all books that have survived in libraries; in practice some major problems have yet to be solved, but so much progress of this sort has been made recently as to encourage guarded optimism.

It is possible that many critics will regard the discussion of short-title catalogues and union catalogues, let alone of their being entered into computers, with distaste. Such lists, however, mechanical though they are, provide historical critics for the first time with systematically prepared access to the displaced literary environment they seek. Further, unlike the displaced social environment, it is virtually intact and any part of it is accessible by means of photography without our even having to travel far for it. A generation ago such resources were simply inconceivable.

The scale of these resources should be noted at this point. To take a single year of the British Library's *Eighteenth-Century Short-Title*

Catalogue as an example, in 1775 approximately 1,732 books were published.[21] The British Library's holdings, though remarkably extensive, are by no means complete, and a union catalogue would increase the number, perhaps even double it. Further, there is an increase in the number of annual publications as one moves towards the present. If one wished, however, to test the literary environment of a work published in 1783, say William Blake's *Poetical Sketches*, by examining the works published during the preceding twenty years, one would have approximately 34,650 titles to survey.[22] There is obviously a risk that even the most devoted historical critics are likely to throw up their hands in despair and complain that having hoped for needles they have been fobbed off with haystacks. Yet despite their size they are finite haystacks and we have never had a clear sight of them before. Our quite natural sense of despair arises from the realization that traditional methods will not work on such massive materials and perhaps from an uneasy realization of how very selectively the present foundations of historical criticism have been prepared.

The crucial elements in the information that is now available, or is at any rate increasingly being made available, are the complete range of evidence and the accessibility of any specified part of it. If we wish to define the displaced literary environment of any period, the necessary materials are for the first time limited, divided from the literary environments of other periods, and present as a whole. To return for a moment to the analogy with botany, the situation is something like that which Linnaeus faced in the eighteenth century when he undertook his comprehensive classification of plants. The field of study is enormous; certain ingrained habits of classification that have preceded this new opportunity will have to be treated sceptically and required to justify themselves all over again in their changed context. But the exhilaration felt at the prospect by the great botanist will be missed by historical critics only if they are unwilling to concede that their work will benefit their successors, that their successors will be wiser than they are, and that reliable conclusions on many of the issues we are used to regarding as most important will not be arrived at for several generations. Such acknowledgements have been the commonplaces of science for centuries and there seems to be no good reason why seekers after literary knowledge should not find satisfaction in the modest role of their individual contributions.

We have the opportunity now to begin a new era in historical criticism, and with such a task ahead it hardly seems to make any difference where one begins. There is obviously more likelihood of progress, however, if priorities can be agreed upon and if our efforts are co-ordinated. Two phases of study seem to be required: one that looks ahead, to some degree speculatively, trying out classifications and relationships having examined the new evidence selectively but with an attempt to choose it representatively; the other examining limited segments of the evidence exhaustively, an enterprise in which many might be involved, their results gradually accumulating and providing a basis for the confirmation, modification, or rejection of the speculative work. Meanwhile there will be no need for gardening to stop; historical critics will still be able to expound the meaning of the literature of the past, but they will do so not only with information more reliably obtained than before but also with a much more realistic sense of the tentative status of their results.

Recovery of the literary environment in historical criticism has so far stressed the parts of it that have survived as elements of the modern literary environment. We are used to allowing for Milton's awareness of Spenser and Shakespeare, and for Fielding's acquaintance with Cervantes or Sterne's with Rabelais. It is as though a dominant literary tradition may be discerned running like a thread through each period which new works draw upon, allude to, or take for granted, often, presumably, without conscious intent.[23] One may complicate this picture somewhat by noting that the elements of the tradition are themselves many-faceted and multi-dimensional and that when they are gathered together they resemble not so much a thread as a gigantic cable of many strands or threads so complicatedly interwoven that many parts of it are for a while invisible, only to emerge to view in their turn, each strand contributing to the strength of the whole and affecting and sometimes interfering with our view of other parts.

What is now being proposed is that the literary tradition so conceived should be placed in juxtaposition with the parts of the literary environment that have not survived as elements of the modern literary environment. The cable of contemporary literature will be less complicatedly interwoven and may be conceived of as passing through the cable of literary tradition in rather the way that ocean currents pass through one another, subsequently becoming temporarily an indistinguishable whole and continuing on their separate courses with undiminished momentum. The historical critic wishes to recover the shared interval of juxtaposition when the new and old, what to later ages will be thought of as the insignificant and the significant, are blended indistinguishably into a literary environment to which new literature may refer. In diagrammatic terms it is tempting to use the image of two lines intersecting, with the literary environment being the point of intersection, but it is important than to conceive of the point of intersection as a massive three-dimensional affair inviting minute examination thread by thread and wholly inimical to impatient generalization.

From a conceptual point of view, exhaustive access to evidence of past literary environments is quite a simple idea; it is the implementation of the new resources that is likely to be laborious, slow, and difficult to pursue efficiently. There are nevertheless one or two further conceptual complications, and it may be that considering them will be of some help in suggesting how the implementation might be carried out.

Even where there are hundreds of thousands of books extant in a defined literary period, many of them will be reprints or new editions, possibly as many as half. Not only does this duplication mean that there is less to be read than there may at first have appeared to be, but it is an invaluable guide to one of the kinds of information most needed by the historical critic, the relative popularity or currency of works. As a rule the repeated publication of a work indicates that the general readership could have been assumed to be familiar with it.[24] It would be quite easy to compile tables of the most often published books decade by decade – the top ten, the top twenty, the top fifty, and so on – and it would be within the capacity of any historical critic, and of any student who aspired to be a historical critic, to read these and by doing so to observe a displaced literary environment in a way that is likely to be representative and relatively free of the influence of the critic's previous expectations. Such reading would provide a sounder basis for generalizations about the literary environments of the past than does our repeated scrutiny of the works of those environments that have retained modern favour.

Duplication apart, many of the books published in a defined period will be survivors from previous eras. In many cases these are works by the very authors whom we would have expected to see – Shakespeare, Milton, etc. – but incidence of republication can often reveal that the relative popularity of great authors has changed, that Shakespeare only gradually overtook Beaumont and Fletcher, for example, or that Milton was for a long time eclipsed by Pope. Further, if the actual works involved are examined it will often be found that the titles most regularly reprinted differ from the titles on which we are accustomed to base the reputation of these authors. To say that Shakespeare is taken for granted by authors from the middle of the eighteenth century is a useful first step; to be able to specify which parts of Shakespeare's canon were taken for granted will be more useful still.

In the short term such crude strategies are likely to modify our knowledge and our experience of displaced literary environments helpfully; the more exact work that remains to be done is by its very nature harder to define in advance. Some of its characteristics, however, seem to be predictable, even if its results cannot be anticipated. The first characteristic is that it will involve the careful reading of groups of books chosen because they belong to a category that is defined in a way free from modern biases (whatever those may be). It would, for instance, be possible to read all the books of a particular publisher for a specific period of time, to classify them, perhaps in a variety of ways – by author, genre, length, sales, presence or absence of illustrations, etc. – and then to attempt some generalizations about them and relate these to current suppositions about the period. Such a topic might even be suitable for thesis writers, and it would certainly provide topics for theses for a long time to come. Many such studies might be thought of as gradually being linked to one another, but categories of books that overlapped with one another would be a useful check on the adequacy of the categories themselves. Some studies of this kind have been attempted in the past but their rareness is indicated by the fact that they are rarely superseded. If this kind of study became widespread, obsolescence would be inevitable, but correspondingly our knowledge of the displaced literary environments would become genuinely progressive.

A further requirement is that we should read books from the displaced literary environment in a way that resembles the way in which they were read when they were new. In a sense this requirement is a circular one; if one reads books from the displaced literary environment in order to read historically it makes no sense to require that one do so by reading historically in the first place. If the capacity for historical reading hoped for at the end of the process were not significantly greater than the capacity one started with, the process would be unnecessary. Nevertheless, having the aim of historical criticism clearly in mind, and remembering too that our modern presuppositions are likely to interfere at various points, should make us more observant and readier to benefit from the fresh evidence we are considering, and in certain respects the tyro may be at an advantage over experienced scholars here both in bringing a 'modern' perspective to bear that is slightly different from the one assumed in published criticism and by being less deeply imbued with hard-won notions of what to expect. It is, in fact, difficult to think of any field in which the opportunities for a young critic are so great for working on fresh evidence and correcting the errors of the intellectual establishment. In 1919 it was possible for astronomers to put Einstein's general theory of relativity to the test of empirical verification by making observations of an eclipse of the sun in Brazil. Einstein is said to have been confident of the results, but it was the verification of the observers that finally broke resistance to his revolutionary view.[25] This expected interplay between theorist and observer is scarcely known in literary criticism. Its lack is usually explained by differences between literature and nature, but it has more to do with the paucity of verifiable observation in the work of critics and the consequent unlikelihood that any theory can ever be proved to be right or wrong.

5

THE RELATIONSHIP OF HISTORICAL CRITICISM TO SOME ALTERNATIVE MODES

> I have found that most of the denominations are right in a large part of what they affirm, but not in so much of what they deny.
>
> Leibniz

In its most comprehensive sense historical criticism plays a part in our reading of all past works of literature, and it contributes to other kinds of criticism even when their practitioners are unsympathetic to its aims and unaware of the extent to which what they regard as common knowledge is ultimately derived from it. In considering the strategies available to historical criticism, however, it seems advisable to consider also ways in which other kinds of criticism may be a help or a hindrance to it. Redefinition of what historical criticism requires at present leads in turn to some unexpected alliances, and it seems likely that critics working remote from one another and for different ends have contrived strategies that are incidentally complementary because they were trying to modify or remove the same obstacle from a different point of view. Those who begin digging tunnels on opposite sides of the same mountain are unlikely to meet unless they do so by prior arrangement, but if by chance they find themselves close to one another though headed in different directions a connecting detour will be of mutual advantage.

In the discussion that follows I have made no attempt to be comprehensive and have concentrated on a small number of representative and influential critical methods, some of which are usually thought of as sympathetic to the historical approach and some unsympathetic. Grouping other critical modes according to their particular bearing on the aims and methods of historical criticism does violence to conventional ways of thinking of them and it is likely to seem unsatisfactory to those who practise them, but, as long as it is understood that they are being viewed selectively from the prejudicing perspective of historical criticism without any intention of interference in their general activity, the temporary distortions involved may be tolerable.[1]

I

Paradoxical though it may seem, one of the most serious obstacles to a reformed historical criticism is traditional literary history. Many modern critics have reacted to its more obvious shortcomings by trying to ignore it, but like our awareness of the past it leaves a residue in the mind, the influence of which is all the more insidious for being set aside rather than re-examined. Literary history has perhaps suffered most from its demonstrated failure to be objective; even where literary historians allowed for or repressed their individual preferences, the assumptions they shared with their contemporaries have given their most impersonal judgements a dated air. Literary history shares this problem with history itself and it seems to be unavoidable; but literary history, because of its stress on the aesthetic merit of its subject matter, has been especially vulnerable to changes of taste. From the point of view of historical criticism, however, traditional literary history is more seriously deficient in its dependence on too narrow a basis of evidence and in its insistence on reaching conclusions that become untenable if the basis of evidence is enlarged substantially or differently defined. One of the conclusions that has proved most damaging to further progress has been the idea that literary periods have an identifiable character that distinguishes them from other literary periods. Like the idea that nations have a character that distinguishes them from other nations, this belief is so widespread as almost to constitute a critical axiom.

The subject matter of literary history, like the subject matter of social history, is even more obviously an uninterrupted continuum than history in general. It may be affected by significant historical events – the fall of Rome, the French Revolution, or the First World War – and it is punctuated by significant literary events – the composition of *Il paradiso*, *Faust*, or *Ulysses* – but the effects of such events on literature are not immediately manifested and they are difficult to trace and to assess even when they appear. Nevertheless, like any large topic, literary history cries out for division into manageable sections. In the academic study of English literature there is widespread agreement on seven: the Anglo-Saxon or Old

English period, petering out some time after the Norman Conquest; the Middle English period, beginning shortly after the Conquest and continuing until the last quarter of the fifteenth century; the Renaissance,[2] beginning with the introduction of movable type in the 1470s and lasting until the end of the Commonwealth in 1660; the Restoration and eighteenth century, lasting from 1660 to 1800; the Romantic period, overlapping somewhat and lasting from 1780 to 1837; the Victorian period, lasting from 1837 to 1901; and the modern period, bringing us up to the present, or as close to the present as the literary historian cares to venture. These sections are useful in such co-operative enterprises as the preparation of bibliographies of modern scholarship; they influence the way in which academic curricula are arranged; and they have a very considerable effect on the boundaries of interest declared by specialists. It will be apparent that the seven periods in question are very unequal if one considers them as blocks of time, amounting to 500, 400, 190, 140, 57, 64, and 88 years respectively.[3] Considered in terms of the extant literature included in them, the steady reduction in the number of years reflects its steady increase, and the faltering of this trend as one comes to the modern period is a reminder that some time has passed since the divisions were reassessed. Examination of the points of division, moreover, reveals a notable lack of consistency. The first period is defined by its distinctive language; the second may be thought of as bringing us up either to the beginnings of modern language or to the beginning of the modern world with the invention of printing. Both divisions make a certain degree of sense if one's interests are etymological (an important consideration in the early days of the academic adoption of English literature) but they are peculiar to the English-speaking world.[4] The third would serve as a turning-point for European literature in general. The division of the third period from the fourth is neither etymologically nor internationally significant. The Restoration of Charles II marks the beginning of a political system that established itself in the United Kingdom in the course of the following century and that may be said to survive still; the division makes sense in terms of British constitutional history. The Romantic period occupied a space between the eighteenth century and the Victorian era, overlapping with the later part of the eighteenth century. To the Victorians who drew up these divisions it was the most recent period before their own, and the reign of the queen and the national and imperial consciousness with which it was associated probably made her accession seem to be a suitable closing date. The Romantic period was distinctive in defining the period of activity of a particular literary movement; as the Victorians have been to us, the Romantics were to the Victorians – those difficult immediate predecessors with whom it was necessary to compare themselves. The two final periods are something of an afterthought and they are the ones that seem most likely to be changed in the near future. Rival divisions (the 'age of transition' 1880–1920, postmodernism, etc.) point to their unsettled nature.

Neither the inconsistency of the ways in which the periods have been arrived at nor inconveniences of the kind experienced by critics of Milton whose author's career is cut in two in 1660 would be very serious, and one might accept the divisions as arbitrary necessities, were it not for two consequences that were not originally bargained for. One is the specialization of critics by period. There are, of course, critics whose specialization is genre or some other category not defined by chronology, and there are critics whose work is not defined by a single language, but on the whole these critics contribute little to historical criticism, however much they may be influenced by its existence. For the many critics who confine their study to one of the periods, the questions that have most often been asked about works in the particular period over the past fifty years tend to seem to be the natural questions to ask and to be different from the questions that are natural to ask in other periods. Sometimes such differences prove fruitful when specialists from one period visit another period and import with them the questions they are used to. The migration of Fredson Bowers from Renaissance drama to eighteenth-century and nineteenth-century fiction, for example, has brought to the later periods the punctiliousness of textual analysis that arose out of the attempt to recover Shakespeare's texts;[5] but the effectiveness of such migrations is an indication that much of the difference between the different techniques common in different periods is an accidental result of the problems encountered by critics rather than a consequence of the distinctive qualities of the texts they were criticizing.

Dividing literature into periods might be accepted as a merely practical convenience, the essential arbitrariness of which could be acknowledged and allowed for were it not for the unnecessary but widespread practice of attributing distinctive characters to them. This practice may have its origin in the desire for a name less cumbersome than, say, 'literature from 1660 to 1800'. As long as the name chosen is one that has a well-established meaning independent of literature – for example, the 'Victorian period' – it may be relatively innocuous; but as soon as it seems to convey a description of the period the drawbacks begin to become apparent. For a long time literature of the eighteenth century was offered to readers by critics and by the compilers of anthologies as the 'age of reason'. But what may once have seemed a rather inviting name to critics was found by teachers to be a forbidding and unsympathetic one to students. Donald Greene's book *The Age of Exuberance* makes a good case for the eighteenth century's being more exuberant than reasonable, and it is probable that exuberance is more likely to appeal to the young. But other summations might be argued for – the 'age of melancholy', say, or, to allow for almost all possibilities, the 'age of variety'. 'The ways of summing up an age depend upon the interests and values of its observers and on the aspects of the age that they observe; the objective reality would not be easy to confirm.

Controversy over an appropriate way of describing English literature of the eighteenth century is mild by comparison with controversy over the usefulness of the word 'Romantic' to describe the period that follows. The difference is probably due to several causes – the term is a foreign one applied originally to other literatures and then imported and applied to English, the number of English authors involved is relatively small, the authors in question are still widely read, and so on – but the most important one seems to be that the word 'Romantic' has been defined in some detail and has been used as a point of departure by much practical criticism of the authors so designated.

The classic confrontation on the subject occurred more than thirty years ago between A.O. Lovejoy and René Wellek. In his well-known essay 'On the discrimination of Romanticisms' Lovejoy pointed out that the terms 'Romantic' and 'Romanticism' were regularly applied to works of literature in ways that were inconsistent and often mutually contradictory:

> The word 'romantic' has come to mean so many things that, by itself, it means nothing. It has ceased to perform the function of a verbal sign. When a man is asked . . . to discuss Romanticism, it is impossible to know what ideas or tendencies he is to talk about, when they are supposed to have flourished, or in whom they are supposed to be chiefly exemplified. (p. 232)

Lovejoy went on to present impressive and sometimes amusing illustrations of the confusion of thought he was referring to and suggested that it would be better to recognize from the start that there was a 'plurality of Romanticisms, of possibly quite distinct thought-complexes, a number of which may appear in one country' (p. 235). Lovejoy focused his attention on inconsistencies in the use of the term rather than on the realities to which the term claimed to point, and in retrospect his essay seems almost playful in its air of being above the battle. However, while he may have regarded the issue as being one more example of intellectual inconsistency, or of an idea that could already be regarded with a degree of historical detachment, to those whose critical work took Romanticism for granted its truth or untruth was a crucial question.

To René Wellek the effect of Lovejoy's remarks was to discourage attempts to arrive at generalizations and to encourage critics to turn instead 'to an investigation of facts and the interpretation of individual poems'.[7] While this prospect even without Lovejoy's intervention might have seemed rather attractive in the 1940s to many critics of English literature, a loss of faith in Romanticism would have been a serious blow for those interested in fostering the study of comparative literature. Whatever its inconsistencies or weaknesses, the concept of Romanticism had provided a powerful alternative to the organization of literature by languages and nationalities. Great things have often been accomplished in the service of muddled creeds, but only while they were not perceived as being muddled. The response of comparative literature, embodied in René Wellek, who was to become one of its most effective spokesmen, was to defend the creed by maintaining that Romanticism was indeed a reality and that 'the major romantic movements form a unity of theories, philosophies, and style, and that these, in turn, form a coherent group of ideas each of which implicates the other' (p. 129). His essay drew for its evidence on a characteristically broad range of European languages far beyond the compass of most modern critics, and its general effect seems to have been to reassure the faithful and confound the sceptics.[8]

Wellek's response to Lovejoy is satisfyingly direct. In the first place he makes it clear that in describing Romanticism he is describing a phenomenon that was dominant 'at a specific time of the historical process' (p. 129). He was not merely pointing to a 'metaphysical entity' or a theme, or to a potentiality of any literature at any time that might be observed in the Romantic period but also in other periods. This historical claim is the ground of subsequent controversy about Romanticism and what distinguishes the conventional meaning of Romanticism from such terms as realism, symbolism, and so on. Wellek conceded Lovejoy's point about the unsatisfactory variety of definitions of Romanticism but proposed that efforts be made to improve the definition. Neither Wellek nor Lovejoy proposed a serious re-examination of the literature in question, and one might well feel that they were exemplifying respectively Locke's dictum about wit and judgement.[9] Whether or not one concludes that their difference of opinion was no more than the difference between two manners of thinking about things, the resolution of the subsequent dispute turns, in the end, on the historical reality or historical unreality of the phenomenon and not on the adequacy of the way in which it has been described.

The confusion to which discussion of the problem is liable may be avoided if we consider a simple analogy about which we feel indifferent. If, for instance, someone asserts that from 1780 to 1835 the majority of English-speaking people were blue-eyed, we know exactly what is meant and can set about finding out whether the assertion is true or false. If records are inadequate we may not be able to find out, but in that case we shall decide that the assertion cannot be proved true or false and will probably not depend much on either alternative as a basis for subsequent argument. If, however, someone asserts that from 1780 to 1835 the majority of English-speaking people were virtuous, there is immediate doubt about what is meant. Regardless of what records may be available we shall be uncertain about what to look for in them. The word 'Romantic' is more like the word 'virtuous' than like the word 'blue-eyed'. If it could be reduced to simpler components such as 'teetotal' or 'preferring the past to the present' some progress might be made, step by step, towards the whole concept of virtue or Romanticism, but until the quality sought is unambiguously defined controversy as to whether it has been found cannot profitably begin. Wellek required seventy pages to present his 'concept of Romanticism' and, though much of his space is devoted to the provision of examples, the definition he arrives at is as rich in complication as in significance. The definition he provided is a challenging problem, not an authoritative solution.

Even on the crucial question of the historical predominance of Romanticism he makes it clear that, when he speaks of 'the prevalence of one set of norms compared with the prevalence of another set in the past', this 'domination' must not be conceived of statistically but rather as of a prevalence among 'writers of greatest artistic importance' (p. 129). At first glance this may seem to be an unexceptionable qualification; after all, we are mainly interested in writers of greatest artistic significance, and literary critics rarely muster enthusiasm for statistics. But if one applies this qualification to our simpler analogy it proves troublesome. If someone asserts that from 1780 to 1835 most people in the English-speaking world were blue-eyed and then insists that this prevalence must not be conceived of statistically but rather as a prevalence among virtuous people, the whole controversy is brought to a standstill. How does one decide which authors are of greatest importance? That the question is far from settled may be seen in Wellek's own difficulties over the case of Goethe, whom he wishes to retrieve from the traditional category of classical: 'All the artistic power of Goethe', he maintains, 'is in the lyrics, in Faust, and in the novels, where there is scarcely any trace of classicism' (p. 162). The prevalence is to be thought of not only as being limited to 'writers of the greatest artistic importance', but as being limited to their works of greatest importance. These conditions are unacceptable on two grounds. In the first place, like 'virtue' and 'Romanticism' the criterion of greatest artistic importance is too complicated, too capable of being differently understood, to provide the basis of any discussion that could lead to proof or disproof. In the second place, the argument appears to be circular. It is impossible to be sure that, consciously or unconsciously, the proponent of Romanticism is not judging works of literature to be of artistic importance because they have 'Romantic' characteristics and then, on putting the important ones together, finding that they all have Romantic characteristics. Whatever our distaste for statistics, the *only* way of establishing the prevalence of a kind of literature in a historical period is by random sample or exhaustive reading of the literature of the period. Until that sort of study is undertaken we shall be obliged to return a Scotch verdict of 'unproven' on Romanticism.

The shortcomings of characterizations of the Romantic period are inherent in any attempt to move from mere labels for historical periods to attempts to sum them up descriptively. They would not be of direct concern to historical criticism were it not that many critics, particularly critics working in the Romantic period, approach individual works of literature supposing that they will or should fulfil the expectations aroused by the characterization.[10] Quite apart from the unresolved question whether or not the expectations are valid, no one has yet claimed that the expectations were in the minds of the original readers of the works. It is essential that modern concepts, true or false, should be forgotten when one is trying to read works as they were read by their original readers. Reading Wordsworth or Byron with a mind full of 'Romanticism' is inimical to historical criticism. As a general rule, the more active the critical effort to generalize about a literary period has been, the greater the handicap to historical criticism. Generalization itself is not incompatible with historical criticism; at present it is merely premature.

II

Evaluation is inseparable from the normal experience of reading. In its least conscious form it is detectable in our preference for the works of one author rather than another, on the 'more of the same' principle, and in our recurrent reading of favourite works. At this level at least taste in art has affinities with taste in food. Private or public communications of our preferences and arguments in favour of them are more self-conscious developments of a common experience. However, because our evaluations, whether they are spontaneous or deliberate, necessarily reflect values – literary, social, etc. – that are derived from our experience of our modern environment, it seems likely that they will hinder attempts to understand literature of the past in so far as they differ from the values that were derived from the environment of the past.

In the long run evaluation seems to be incompatible with historical criticism. If we are to read works of past literature as they were read when they were new it will be helpful if we can suspend our habit of approving or disapproving for a while, even if, in the end, our historical criticism leads us to make up our minds in a historically informed way. The desirability of disinterested reading in the historical critic is not just that it may contribute to a more 'objective' body of criticism upon which even those of other persuasions will be able to rely,[11] but that the activity of modern values is likely to interfere with our perception of the values of the past. It may be argued, with considerable justice, that objectivity in the sense we associate with a controlled scientific experiment is inconsistent with the act of reading a work of literature, but if we make an effort to allow for the intrusion of the values peculiar to our time and to be alert to the existence of values peculiar to an earlier period, especially if we practise the effort until it becomes a largely unconscious habit, we are likely to avoid the excesses of anachronism.

Quite apart from the artificiality of disinterested reading, however, it is extremely difficult to become conscious of the anachronistic values one imports into the past, and certain kinds of criticism that stress approval or disapproval in an attempt to reform modern values seem to be useful as ways of dislodging or at least revealing values that are so entrenched in the modern environment that we are unaware that they are neither necessary nor permanent. This process of dislodgement has something in common with the medical practice of homoeopathy in which physical disorders are treated by the administration of small doses of drugs that in healthy people produce similar symptoms. For criticism that is determinedly evaluative to have this curative effect, it seems to be necessary that its values be those of a group rather than of an individual. The values of groups are articulated first by individuals, but if they are to have any weight the experience of the individual must be acknowledged as representative by others.[12] It is not that what is recognized by the group is 'truer' than what is recognized by the individual, but rather that the experience of a group that is at odds with the experience of most of their contemporaries provides, once it has been expressed, an alternative or rival contemporary environment. The social environment to which literature refers will differ from the social environment taken for granted by the majority, and as the group becomes established it will begin to refer to a distinctive literary environment as well. It is not necessary that the values of the group should prevail over the values of the majority – indeed, if they did their helpfulness to the cause of historical criticism would cease; it is enough if they can present a consistent and rich alternative that makes the majority conscious of the relativeness of its own values.

The effectiveness of criticism that stresses values is directly related to the presence of unexamined values in traditional criticism. The confrontation of one set of values with another is not of itself particularly rewarding to the historical critic, but it may be looked upon as an intermediary stage preparing the way for more useful developments.

Evaluation as a critical aim is accessibly exemplified in the influential criticism of F.R. Leavis. Leavis's criticism is sometimes represented as being merely opinionated, and when the opinions he expresses are controversial or novel the bluntness of his manner of expression is apt to make unsympathetic readers opinionative in response; but his intention, and his practice when he is not being harried by controversy, is evaluative in a painstaking and responsible way.[13] For Leavis, evaluation in criticism is not a matter of arriving at a set of values and then applying them consistently to works of literature,[14] nor is it one of identifying and stating unexplored and spontaneous preferences. Indeed, evaluation as he conceives of it has the complexity of a total social confrontation between reader and text; it can be described only by means of its symptoms and recognized only by having been experienced. Leavis's insistence on evaluation – 'You cannot be intelligent about literature without judging' (p. 89) – may be looked upon as a return to the moral awareness of criticism prior to the aestheticism and 'art for art's sake' assumptions of the turn of the century, or even as a repudiation of Arnold's recommendation that criticism should be 'disinterested',[15] but the moral assumptions that he and his followers brought to bear were sufficiently different from those that had lain dormant for half a century to have an air of revolution rather than of revival.

The revolution, such as it was, nevertheless was not wholly of Leavis's making. His own experience of going from a provincial middle-class background to an academic and critical establishment whose values were based on a different experience of life was shared by an increasing proportion of readers in the next two generations. For Leavis's generation the choice for such readers was between allowing oneself to be assimilated into a dominant social minority and suppressing one's provinciality and adopting cosmopolitan attitudes on the one hand, and, on the other, being obliged to reassess the whole literary tradition for oneself. Even those most sympathetic to Leavis seem to me to make too little of the daunting nature of the latter prospect; but once Leavis had led the way, especially as a lecturer at Cambridge, the need he had felt that literature was not to be separated from one's personal experience and attached instead to an assumed corporate experience was responded to eagerly by other provincial readers from other towns and other countries.[16]

Leavis's most lasting contribution to critical practice seems likely to be his success in persuading readers to make up their own minds about texts and in showing them how much that entails if it is to be done responsibly. But even when the response to his example has been merely to adopt his conclusions, instead of adopting the conclusions of his predecessors, the effect has been useful, from the point of view of historical criticism, in changing or at least challenging an established literary canon. Where Leavis and his followers have, perhaps, been less active than their cause suggests they might be is in the recovery of authors whom the earlier literary establishment simply ignored. Leavis himself was active in seeking out and recognizing talent among his contemporaries, but he does not seem to have faced the implication of the long prevalence of 'false' values as a determinant of our knowledge of the literature of the past. From the point of view of historical criticism, however, the rise of a conflicting series of evaluations and the modifications of the traditional canon are useful evidence of the relativity of literary values and of the changes that take place in them as time passes. As more and more provincial readers, and readers from other provinces, assimilate Leavis's lessons directly or indirectly, the evaluations and the canon that reflect them seem likely to continue to undergo change. The academic habit of avoiding evaluation has contributed to the supposition that evaluation is only a matter of personal idiosyncrasy; to be shown that a single large group of intelligent and committed readers can bring quite different values to bear on literature from those brought to bear by other large groups among their contemporaries is a small step away from considering it likely that groups divided from one another by centuries will differ even more drastically.

Leavis's evaluations were founded on values that while left largely inexplicit had a consistency and coherence that depended upon his habitual outlook on life. The persuasiveness of these evaluations depended, in turn, upon their being recognized and approved by readers whose habitual outlook on life had much in common with his. What began as the expression of an individual was given weight by being sanctioned by a group. Leavis's mode remains inescapably personal, however, and to criticize as he does at his best requires that the critic forget the group that may or may not sanction the results. Marxist criticism, by contrast, begins with the sanction of the group.

Marxist criticism grows out of the Marxist view that the economy and its organization determine social phenomena.[17] Presumably traditional criticism also arose from assumptions that were not primarily aesthetic, let alone literary, but those assumptions were not explicitly embraced by traditional critics and have to be disentangled afterwards with some difficulty from the criticism that took them for granted. Marxist criticism has the advantage of offering a non-literary theory in advance of a deliberately consequent literary practice. Furthermore, the non-literary theory is a way of perceiving the social environment that differs from the prevailing way of perceiving the social environment. In a sense, the convinced Marxist who reads non-Marxist literature in a non-Marxist society is referring literature to a perceived environment that is quite like what we have called a displaced social environment. The effect of this reference is to find weaknesses in much literature that has traditionally been regarded as central and to give unusual prominence to some works that give what from a Marxist standpoint is a more representative or worthwhile account of their social environment. From the point of view of historical criticism the considerable success of Marxist criticism is unexpectedly helpful. The very fact that critics should be made aware that substantial numbers of their contemporaries experience the modern social environment in ways that differ from their own experience alerts their imaginations to the existence of alternative perceptions that are not merely bloodless historical reconstructions; it also makes it seem probable that our perceptions of our social environment are subject to change. Having observed the differences of outlook in our contemporaries, we are likely to expect or at least consider the possibility of such differences of outlook in our predecessors. If we draw back at the results of a thoroughgoing Marxist interpretation of, say, Shakespeare's plays, we should be more amenable to considering the possibility that a thoroughgoing modern interpretation of them will also be misconceived; and, if the thought does not occur to us spontaneously, Marxist criticism is likely to draw it to our attention. The Marxist approach to literary criticism is probably the most powerful example we have of the operation of a way of thinking that seems alien to non-Marxists but seems natural to substantial numbers of their contemporaries who share the same social environment. If such differences are possible when the environment is the same, how much more likely they were when it was different, before the environment was displaced by the passage of time!

The differences between Marxist criticism and traditional criticism are so fundamental that the resources of traditional criticism have turned out to be unsatisfactory for Marxists and have required to be replaced. Because traditional bibliographies have taken for granted the value of a comparatively small group of authors,[18] a value arrived at on the assumptions of traditional criticism, it has seemed acceptable to record and keep accessible the work of this group and to omit the writings of the vastly larger majority of writers as being comparatively insignificant. This procedure is sensible enough – there have been too many writers for us to attend to all or most of them – as long as the criterion for inclusion in the smaller group is common ground. But Marxist critics are bound to be suspicious and may well wish to review the work of the many in a Marxist spirit, expecting to come upon authors overlooked or suppressed by traditional criticism. This review overlaps with one of the tasks of historical criticism. The interest of Marxist criticism in the less sophisticated forms of literature – ballads, chapbooks, broadsheets, penny dreadfuls, yellow books, and the like – is hampered by the ephemeral nature of such work, but may nevertheless make significant advance in the face of imperfect or scanty evidence by sheer dint of caring enough about the subject.

The Marxist interest in the economic side of life has led to an examination of literature as a commodity, stressing its dependence on a market and the influence of that dependence on the author as worker and de-emphasizing the individual contribution of the author in favour of the concept of author as representative spokesman. It is not the purpose of this interest to undermine the presupposition of the creative and inspired individual, but that is its effect; and by expecting the worker (the author) to be one worker among many it is disinclined to separate his or her work from the work of more obscure contemporaries. As a result the literary environment of past authors seems once more to be of interest. The economics of literature, like the economics of nursery gardening or of cotton-spinning, involves not only the labour of the producers but also the contribution of those who prepare the products for the market and those who market them. In literary terms, publishers, printers, and booksellers[19] become of interest as the means of production and distribution, and there is an incentive to investigate them that is similar in effect to the incentive there was among editors of Shakespeare's texts to investigate the methods of book production of the Elizabethan period.

Any group that advocates reform has an interest in evidence that our current ways of doing or perceiving things are neither absolute nor immutable. The Marxist interest in the past fits this pattern, as Marxist historians point to alternative methods and alternative institutions in earlier periods as a way of demonstrating that our modern capitalist methods and institutions are the products of temporary conditions and temporary needs. At its best (from a historical critic's point of view) the Marxist expectation (and hope) that the future will involve a change from the present presupposes that the present differs in its turn from the past. Added to this insistence on the idea of difference in the past is the belief that the activities of individuals are not separable from the societies in which the individuals live and are indeed to a large extent determined by their societies. This belief is usually categorized in political terms, but it runs so directly counter to the prevailing post-Romantic axiom that great art is the work of inspired individuals that it takes on an aesthetic importance as well. As an aesthetic belief this view was given currency by Hegel and predates Marxism, but the coupling of a political and social dimension to it has allowed it to revive as a countervailing view.

As a consequence of their personal experience, Marxist critics are likely to be aware of the phenomenon of the displaced environment and are likely to make non-Marxists aware of it too. Like historical critics, although for reasons that are initially different, Marxist critics are interested in the social fabric of the past and inclined to be suspicious of the transcendent position in it accorded by modern taste to a few literary figures. Like historical critics, Marxist critics are interested in establishing the norms of the past and resist exclusive attention to the exceptions no matter how admirable the exceptions may seem. There appears to be a natural alliance between these two kinds of critics that might well be exploited to their mutual advantage. The appearance of what has begun to be called the 'New Historicism' suggests that this opportunity is beginning to be recognized.[20]

Feminist criticism has affinities with both Leavis's kind of criticism and Marxist criticism,[21] since it seeks an understanding of literature that does not require women to read in ways that de-emphasize their experience as women and usually claims that the experience of women has something in common that differentiates it from the experience of men and hence from the experience that has been taken for granted by a traditional criticism practised mainly by men. It is also similar in significant ways to what may be called nationalist criticism, in which criticism of American literature may be taken as a familiar and well-established example.[22] There are three essential ingredients: first, the realization that the point of view of a group of readers that has begun to define itself or to become conscious of itself as being different from the group to which the established canon of literature has seemed to address itself is a distinctive one; second, that a new canon is drawn up of literature produced by writers who shared what seem to be representative aspects of the experience of the group and referred to them or took them for granted or repressed them in their writing; third, that new literature is evaluated according to criteria similar to those used in drawing up the new canon.[23] In theory the experience of women should be closer to a universal experience than the experience of Americans, but as with the experience of Americans it will be very difficult to identify its most lasting and essential qualities, especially if, as is often the case, feminist criticism goes hand in hand with Marxist criticism and nationalist criticism.

From the point of view of historical criticism, however, the current vitality of feminist criticism is particularly useful. The revaluation of the canon that was one of the preoccupations of Leavis does not serve feminist critics so well, even if his stress on George Eliot was a common bond; a new canon has to be discovered.[24] The most promising place to look for it has been in fiction from the eighteenth century on, a field that criticism was aware of even before Leavis, and one in which women seem to have been active because they could make a living as novelists, albeit a modest one, by the equivalent of cottage industry. Feminist criticism and the feminist movement have made conveniently accessible many books by women that even ten years ago were hard to come by, and some critics have been drawing attention to the popular fiction that not only provided a livelihood for women who wrote but constituted a major part of the fiction read by men and women alike.[25] The effect of this sort of study is to provide a new awareness of a neglected literary environment of past literary works.[26] The exploration of such literature, the more popular the better, is one of the best opportunities we have of recovering some of the literary environment referred to by the works that have traditionally been admired. To reconstitute the canon in such a way that women's writing is adequately represented is more difficult in fields other than fiction, but, at least after the middle of the seventeenth century, it is simply a matter of patient (or devoted) persistence, complicated at times by the recourse of women to anonymity or male pseudonyms. What will be found will form a controlled segment of the material that historical criticism needs to assess.

The re-examination of a neglected literary environment apart, feminist criticism has shown an especially sympathetic interest in the literary presentation of the aspects of life experienced by women. Some of these aspects have traditionally excluded men in western society, just as some aspects of men's experience have traditionally excluded women, but, while it is probably true that more of the established canon of literature has referred to exclusively male experience of the social environment than to exclusively female experience, the preponderance since the Renaissance seems to have concentrated on experience shared by both men and women.[27] In so far as the distinctive perspective of women on shared experience has been insufficiently recognized by critics whose perspective was distinctively male, it seems likely that an examination from the perspective of women will be corrective, and because part at least of that perspective is derived from greater experience of domestic life and a greater stake in family and community relations it is likely to bear particularly upon the nature of the social environment and to provide us with information of the kind that institutional archives have typically ignored.

Both Marxist and feminist critics share the difficulty of identifying the people whose cause they are arguing for; anonymity is a natural consequence of obscurity. This problem is an advantage in disguise, however, in that the critic is not distracted from either the literary or the social environment by the fascinating but often irrelevant details of the lives of authors. Lacking them, attention can be paid instead to the experience that authors shared with readers – the experience that they presume upon in writing books for readers, and the experience that determined what literary works meant to their readers when they were new. Since this is exactly what historical criticism wants to achieve, it seems possible that a useful alliance might be effected.

The service done to the cause of historical criticism by the evaluative modes of modern criticism goes beyond an uneasy congruity of aims and methods, however. For historical critics who are not Marxists or feminists or followers of Leavis, the experience of encountering an elaborately articulated perspective on our social and literary environment that differs from their own, especially if they encounter one perspective after another, is the closest they come to experiencing the sense of strangeness that we would experience if we could be transported into the past. With so much in common, such historical critics may feel, how extraordinary it is that so much should affect other critics differently and how extraordinary that they should feel so strongly. Historical critics who have not had that experience of alienation with the period of the past in which they are most interested have not yet brought it to life. Historical criticism, in turn, may be able to serve the evaluative modes by demonstrating to them that people whose place in society in the past resembles the place of the modern evaluator may nevertheless not have perceived the experience of that place in the same way.[28]

III

I have argued that historical criticism emphasizes the relationship of individual works of literature of the past to the social and literary environments of the past, and that it has much in common with modes of criticism that find it unsatisfactory to separate works of literature from one another as if they could be understood in isolation. Two modes of criticism that have been most influential in this respect, at least in the English-speaking world – Frye's archetypal criticism and structuralism – differ from historical criticism in their procedures and results in ways that run counter to its requirements. In each case, the opposition appears to be unintentional, arising from indifference or unawareness rather than from any underlying disagreement or essential incongruity, and the relationship between these modes of criticism and historical criticism seems to be potentially one of co-operation.

I have already noted the scientific ambitions of the critical approach expounded by Frye in *The Anatomy of Criticism* and his call for critical analysis that forgoes the subjectiveness of evaluation (see pp. 1–2 above). What is even more characteristic of *The Anatomy*, however, is its attempt at categorization of literature as a whole in terms of modes, symbols, myths, and genres of which individual works may be considered as exemplars. Frye's procedure has had great success as a teaching device, complementing New Critical analysis by its insistence upon the interrelatedness of all parts of literature and encouraging advanced students to acquaint themselves with a catholic range of the great works of world literature, and it has been persuasively applied by Frye himself, whose acuteness of analysis and demotic trenchancy of expression are as remarkable in their way as is his hard-won literary systematization.[29]

What Frye claimed to offer in *The Anatomy of Criticism* was, first of all, an argument in favour of 'a synoptic view of the scope, theory, principles, and techniques of literary criticism' and, as a 'secondary aim', 'a tentative version of it' (p. 3). It is important to preserve the two aims distinct from one another and not to limit the possibilities of the first to the actualities of the second. From the point of view of historical criticism *The Anatomy* provides an extraordinarily rich demonstration of the ways in which literary works are written and read in relationship to a literary environment. Since it was the literary environment rather than the social environment that was most conspicuously ignored in 1957, it was reasonable for Frye to emphasize it and for him to de-emphasize the social environment which in the 1950s was widely understood to be the personal experience of the author. Of the social environment as we have defined it, Frye has little to say in *The Anatomy*, although in other works, most notably perhaps in his collection of annual surveys of Canadian poetry, *The Bush Garden*, he is obviously keenly alive to its presence in contemporary literature.[30]

Readers of *The Anatomy of Criticism* are usually struck by the enormous range of the literary environment to which Frye is able to refer. This range may be accepted simply as exemplary, and in that sense it seems to be highly satisfactory. In three other respects it deserves further examination. The first is its relationship to literature as a whole. Enormous though the range is, it constitutes a very small fraction of the literature that exists. The question may therefore be asked: on what principle is the fraction chosen and does that principle determine the categories that are subsequently deduced in ways that might make them less true to fractions chosen on other principles? Frye is not explicit about his choices, but he appears to have read works that have been regarded as significant by literary historians and anthropologists of the past century;[31] the representativeness of such a fraction of the whole could only be tested by systematic reading of surviving literature by teams of readers. Frye's survey in this respect may be regarded as a scientific hypothesis based on a very promising but not yet verified range of evidence that will be tested gradually and that may receive further refinements or modifications in the process. The question being posed here would be whether or not Frye's categories are adequate to the range of literature and representative of it.

The second aspect of Frye's account of the literary environment that needs to be examined critically is its assumption that literature, unlike the past, remains extant as a whole, relatively impervious to time.[32] I have argued above (pp. 36–61) that, although we tend to read works of literature as if they were exempt from the passage of time and tend to value them in so far as they seem to make sense in terms of our own experience, our doing so distorts the works in unforeseeable ways.[33] The meaning of works of literature is altered by a change in the social environment, and so is the relative significance of the works themselves. For the historical critic it will be necessary to refine upon Frye's procedure by identifying the parts of a total literature that constituted the literary environment of the particular work being criticized; in most cases it seems likely that many of the significant works that Frye takes into account would have to be set aside as irrelevant and that many works so insignificant that he does not consider them at all would have to be included.

The third respect in which Frye's presentation of the literary environment requires modification for historical criticism is related to the first. His literary environment is not big enough to be equivalent to literature as a whole, but it is too big to be equivalent to the literary environment that might be supposed to have been familiar to the readers of past works of literature when the works were new. Here what is needed is a careful examination of the literary environment of the particular work being criticized. Once it has been identified, consisting usually of a combination of works new and old, it should, by definition, be fairly easy to become thoroughly acquainted with it.

Archetypal criticism may be thought of as a prophetic view of the kind of knowledge about literature we might eventually have if literature were studied systematically and exhaustively. In this sense it is one of the most powerful allies available to the historical critic and one that has contributed to making an improved historical criticism conceivable. Current applications of archetypal criticism may be regarded as ways of testing the adequacy of the theory, but as far as contributing to historical criticism is concerned they are premature. The literary environment and social environment are not yet sufficiently well established to support them, and the efforts of historical critics to establish them may be thought of as empirical field studies that will gradually accumulate to the point where the prophetic foretaste may be modified by experience.

When Frye's theory is applied to individual works of literature its characteristic feature is the recognition of aspects of the work that are described in his system of literary classification and that have been overlooked because they were not expected to be significant. These aspects sometimes reveal similarities between works usually thought to be too heterogeneous for comparison (between Leporello in *Don Giovanni* and P.G. Wodehouse's Jeeves, for example); sometimes they help us to recognize the presence of elements in the work that had not been noticed before but that, once noticed, seem to be important. In his discussion of *The Winter's Tale*, his analogy between the cycle of the seasons from spring to winter and the cycle of human life from childhood to age prompts him to observe not only the opposing parallels of, on the one hand, age, winter, and jealousy and, on the other, of youth, summer, and love, but also to consider that the unusual lapse of sixteen years in the middle of the play accommodates the slower pace of the human cycle. Here the expectation of a recurrent literary pattern leads to a plausible explanation of two unusual features that had not previously been associated with one another.[34]

The usefulness of Frye's kind of criticism as a practical instrument has much in common with what has come to be called structuralism, a critical activity that, by concentrating on the presence in a literary work of elements that are not apparently related to its meaning, reveals aspects of the meaning that had escaped detection.[35] Frye confines his attentions to the literary environment, while structuralism characteristically relates individual works to wholes such as language or society that exist outside literature and of which literature is only a part. The assumptions of structuralism are indeed so remote from conventional literary concerns that it seems that, while works of literature may furnish it with convenient material to investigate, there is little likelihood that the results will improve our understanding of the individual works.[36] Nevertheless, the impact of structuralist analysis of familiar works has been considerable, in part because, unlike most literary criticism, it is systematic and verifiable and can be easily and deliberately learned, and in part because its results are so drastically variant from those of previous criticism.

Structuralists do not usually show much awareness of the effect of the passage of time on the works they analyse, and they seem at first glance to be working at cross-purposes with historical criticism, but they resemble the evaluative critics in that the shocks they administer to traditional criticism are directed to points in it that historical criticism finds least satisfactory. Structuralists typically bypass apparent meaning in literary works, focusing instead upon latent structures;[37] apparent meaning, as we have seen, is the greatest obstacle to our understanding past works of literature as they were understood when they were new, and, while latent structures cannot be counted on to lead us directly towards such understanding, their aptness for making us relinquish a conventional interpretation temporarily amid a welter of hitherto unthought-of considerations is potentially useful. Structuralists typically show little or no interest in either the social or the literary environments of works of literature, but the social and literary environments that they ignore are the modern ones that are mistakenly taken for granted in unhistorical criticism. Unlike the New Criticism, which gave the impression of ignoring social and literary environments but really depended upon modern ones without explicit acknowledgement, structuralist critics, coming from fields such as linguistics or anthropology, have been able to read literary works with an eye that if not quite innocent seems at least to be innocent of conventional literary expectations. In their place are expectations, linguistic or anthropological, that are unfamiliar to literary critics and that are too coherent in their own terms to be lightly brushed aside. Claude Lévi-Strauss's investigation of incest prohibitions in primitive societies, for example, led him to observe a recurrent connection between incest and puzzle-solving that he is able to apply to the Oedipus legend and that may be readily extended to *Hamlet*.[38] Furthermore, the obvious defence against such innovation requires that literary assumptions about the social and literary environments be made explicit, with the probability that as a consequence critics will disagree about them and seek some way of resolving their disagreement and in doing so are likely to invoke the criterion of original meaning.

Structuralism performs one further service for historical criticism in its lack of interest in the comparative value of works of literature. Structural analysis is just as effective when applied to trash as it is when it is applied to major works and much less likely to give offence, partly because it does not confront entrenched opinion and partly because traditional critics will be novice readers of it too.[39] The advantages of this independence of the merit of the material are most obvious when a large number of works are being compared, especially if they are drawn from a specified historical period. Such studies, for quite different motives, can do much to revive the literary environment to which the historical critic so badly needs access.

IV

The interest of literary criticism in readers (or in audiences) has traditionally been focused on the social consequences of the ways in which readers are changed for better or worse by the experience of reading. The preference of New Critics and formalists for concentrating on the analysis of texts and excluding social consequences as irrelevant seems to have made it easier to consider reading as a process and not merely as a means to a result. 'Reader-response' criticism has been approached from two quite different directions: from the starting-point of the text which seemed, even when considered abstractly, to require the co-operation of a reader to complete it; and from the starting-point of the subjective experience of the individual reader.

The approach that began by considering the text was developed in Poland by Roman Ingarden in the 1930s and did not begin to have much influence in the English-speaking world until the early 1970s. Ingarden's contribution to reader-response criticism began as an attempt to analyse the literary work objectively. He ruled out of bounds any consideration of the role of the author, of the value of the work, of the environment to which it referred, and of the 'attributes, experiences, or psychic states' of the reader.[40] This isolation of the text as the topic for examination was in keeping with the formalist assumptions that prevailed in eastern Europe at the time and with their counterpart in the New Criticism, and the enthusiasm for an objective, almost scientific method finds an analogy in the early work of I.A. Richards. Although in a broad sense Ingarden's contribution can be recognized as symptomatic of its time, it was distinctive in being unwaveringly systematic, insisting on consistency and comprehensiveness.

Ingarden maintained that a literary work is made up of 'heterogeneous strata' that are combined in an 'organic structure', and he identified and classified these strata and explained how they worked.[41]

But the exhaustive ambition of his procedure forced him to concede that something was still missing from his account, and he introduced the concept of 'places of indeterminacy' (his simple example was of the unspecified colour of a character's eyes in a novel). He was then obliged to consider how a reader copes with these places of indeterminacy and to conclude that, while many (like the eye colour) may be left undetermined, others are provided by readers with determinacies of their own. Recognition of the essential role of the reader in bringing a text 'to life' led him to analyse the nature of the reader's contribution or, as he called it, 'concretization'.[42]

Ingarden's acknowledgement of the necessary role of the reader is all the more impressive because it seems to have been forced upon him contrary to his expectation and in spite of his original decision to ignore it. Its current influence, however, stems from its usefulness as a precedent for the application of reader-response criticism to individual texts. Wolfgang Iser, for example, redefines Ingarden's concretization as a dynamic tension between the two poles of text and reader (the chief alteration here being that the reader is accorded a status more nearly equal to that of the text), the reader's imaginative contribution combining with the author's (in so far as the text represents it) to produce the 'virtuality' of the work of literature (p. 275). The active part played by readers in eliciting meaning from texts has been insisted upon and described in simple terms in the explanation of the triangle of literary interpretation in chapter 1 (pp. 23–32), an explanation that is generally compatible with Ingarden's Iser's variant, however, is more troublesome. Ingarden, as we have seen, excluded the environment of a text from his consideration at the outset; Iser carries this exclusion a significant step further by declaring that literary texts 'do not correspond to any objective reality outside themselves' (p. 276). What for Ingarden is a convenient way of limiting the field of enquiry becomes in Iser's hands a matter of fact. Perhaps 'correspond' is the word at fault. It is true that the 'reality' represented in works of literature is not, for the most part, identical with 'objective reality', but it must correspond to it, resemble or differ from it in recognizable ways, otherwise we shall not be able to understand the text no matter how imaginative our reading may be. The triangle of literary interpretation will not work if the apex that stands for the environment is omitted. That important reservation aside, Iser's practical examinations of the ways in which particular texts require and indeed sometimes explicitly invite our imaginative co-operation provide graphic illustrations of what the act of reading entails.

The influence of reader-response criticism that begins by reflecting upon the experience of the individual reader seems to be derived from Norman Holland's *The Dynamics of Literary Response* of 1968. In retrospect the book now seems to be an odd mixture of New Criticism and Freudian psychology, but its most refreshing innovations were Holland's confident reliance on his personal experience of literary works, his willingness to share it without tidying it up first, and his assumption that his experience, *mutatis mutandis*, was representative of the experience of others. By violating critical decorum in this way he relieved criticism of a longstanding inhibition and made it clear that the pallid abstractions of critical theory should not be mistaken for the rich and unpredictable experiences of real readers. Holland has continued to develop this kind of criticism with an increasingly idiosyncratic note (observing, for example, that the word 'purloined' in the title of Poe's *The Purloined Letter* is Norman French 'or, if you like, Norm's French'), but in doing so he makes no claims for the specific particulars of his experience, but rather for the presence of similar 'irrelevant' particulars in the literary experience of each of us.[43]

Together the text-based and reader-based varieties of reader-response criticism have done much to make us aware of what is involved when we read a work of literature that is new, but they show hardly any awareness of the implications of their findings for our attempts to read old works as they were read when they were new. The problem of displaced environment is ignored because environment is generally taken for granted. But a quite different question remains to be asked. Setting aside for the moment the matter of the environment, was the act of reading in the past identical to the act of reading with which we are familiar from our own immediate experience? Certain gross differences between the literary experience of the past and the literary experience of the present are so familiar as to have lost interest for us. We know, for example, that many nineteenth-century novels were issued in weekly parts and that there was some incentive to leave the action of each part interestingly unresolved 'to be continued in our next'. Critics are used to explaining such narrative peculiarities by referring to the original conditions of publication, but generally by way of assisting the modern reader to make allowances rather than with any expectation of recovering the experience of the original readers. Issuing a novel in parts may explain the episodic quality of *The Old Curiosity Shop*, but what difference must it have made to the reader (or listener) to follow the action of the novel for more than a year and a half in weekly instalments? And, while an author's direct remarks to part of his or her potential audience (Dickens's 'If our observant lady readers can deduce any satisfactory inference from these facts, we beg them by all means to do so' in *Pickwick Papers*, for example) may seem gratuitous when read silently in solitude, they take on a different quality when read aloud, as they must have been expected to be, to a mixed company or a family circle. We are used to making a special effort to imagine plays in performance, but should we not do as much for medieval poetry, for Chaucer's *Troilus and Criseyde*, for example, and to regard what can readily be understood by listening to a reading of it as being more crucial than niceties that can be wrung from repeated rereadings of a printed text?

These familiar changes in the external circumstances of the act of reading are probably taken into account already by historical critics, but the aspects of reading brought to our attention by reader-response criticism have hardly begun to be integrated into the historical approach. Ingarden's places of indeterminacy are to be found in all literary works, old as well as new, but when modern readers begin to provide their own determinacies these are bound to differ in unexpected ways from the determinacies of their contemporaries but in more calculable ways from the determinacies of the readers of the old works when they were new. The consequences to the displaced environment are considerable, even when the environment is referred to explicitly; when it is left undetermined and readers are called upon to complete it, they are challenged to provide determinacies from the displaced environment that the literary work could once take for granted. At the other end of the scale, when a critic such as Holland reminds us of the idiosyncratic detail that is part of the experience of reading for every reader, he implies that readers of the past were as idiosyncratic too.[44] While we may be content as readers of contemporary works to observe that we are idiosyncratic and to accept that the condition is normal, there none the less seems to be an obligation, from the point of view of historical criticism at least, to consider the nature of the idiosyncratic elements of reading in the past. Much of what Holland describes in his account of his reading of Poe, for example, is unique to him, but his recollection of having first encountered *The Purloined Letter* as a paperback bound in 'Perma-Gloss', his association of Vienna with 'intrigue', his notion of the struggle between Dupin and the Minister D—— as 'an Oedipal one between father and son', are associations he expects will have a counterpart in our own experience; together they form an acceptable if slightly high-spirited representation of what happens when a modern person reads an old literary work. Can one make any progress towards retrieving a comparable representation of what might have happened when Poe's original readers read *The Purloined Letter*? And, if that challenge to the historical critic is too great, is it possible to make progress by way of what we have referred to earlier as negative certainty and by maintaining that some widely shared modern associations fail to take into account the displaced environment and are simply incongruous?

Deconstruction is not derived from the theory of reader-response criticism, but it is closely related to its application. In each the focus of attention is shifted from the text to what the reader (or critic) does with the text. The text is not ignored and is often and delicately referred to, but it seems to be thought of as the raw material out of which a hitherto unrealized literary work is created.

If one thinks of deconstruction as a form of post-structuralism – that is, as a way of thinking that defines itself as in some way modifying the assumptions and procedures of structuralism – the central point at issue appears to be the nature of language. The structures of structuralist criticism are often derived from analogies in the structure of language, and if one questions the validity of our traditional perception of the structures of language it follows that one will question the critical structures derived from them. As was pointed out in chapter 1 (pp. 12–14 above), in the English-speaking world the traditional perception of the structures of language has been based on two assumptions. The first was that utterances (speech acts) are the result of an utterer (speaker) using words (signifiers) that stand for things or thoughts (signifieds) in order to share with a hearer what is in the utterer's mind. The second assumption was that the relationship between things or thoughts and the words that stood for them was an absolute and consistent one analogous to the relationship once supposed to exist in the mind of God between his thoughts and his utterances. Some of the changes that have taken place in our way of thinking about language are a consequence, ultimately, of the decay of the second assumption.

The causes of the decay seem to have been both philosophical and social. In philosophical terms it has become usual, following upon the attack upon human access to transcendental knowledge carried out by Kant at the end of the eighteenth century, to restrict our enquiries to the actual, even if we admit the possibility or imaginability or even the usefulness of an ideal reality. At the social level, thinking about what the world must be like from God's point of view and indeed thinking of God as possessing thoughts and a personality seem gradually to have receded from being a norm to being an easily recognized exception. The consequences of these changes for the theory of language were not anticipated, language being very much a side issue by comparison with God and the absolute, but the effect of weakening the second assumption has been to leave the first open to question. It was no longer so obvious that one had to assume that a speaker was matching thoughts to words and transferring the thoughts to a listener. Language was still examined, however, on the assumption that it was efficient or at least internally consistent, even if the expectation was derived more from Darwinian notions of evolution than from faith in God. It is the questioning of this residual assumption that lies at the root of deconstruction.

It is the resulting practices of deconstruction, however, rather than its origins or rationale that are of direct concern to historical criticism. Once language is perceived (rightly or wrongly) as being necessarily fixed neither in its ultimate meanings nor in its internal relations, texts, and especially literary texts, seem to float free from their determining or limiting relationships. The one determinant that remains is the reader for whom the text is an occasion for arriving at a meaning but is no longer an agreed-upon restraint upon the meaning arrived at. From the point of view of literary criticism there seem to be potential awkwardnesses to this state of affairs, but it is not without precedent in other areas of human activity.

In the first place, while the decline of reliance on God as a criterion for human ethical behaviour may have led to fears of ethical anarchy or at least general ethical decline, it is not obvious that human behaviour is worse on the whole than it was 300 or 800 years ago. The excesses of intellectuals who feel required to act upon the unappetizing consequences of speculative reasoning in order to show their superiority over common sense have in the past turned out to be exceptions (for instance, the 'actes gratuites' in Gide's *Les Caves du Vatican*). New freedoms are usually overdone for a while. In the second place, the ability of a sensitive critic to see in a text what has not been seen before, to bring out its potentiality, is one of the qualities for which critics have been honoured in the past. Even when a critic's perception is only partially adopted, it is usual to pass over the rejected parts in forgiving silence – Aristotle himself has been granted this privilege.

The historical critic confronted by deconstruction may want to hold on firmly to the historical determinants (the displaced social and literary environments, which have been left untouched by deconstructive critics[45]) as criteria by which to assess interpretative results, but in general the unsettling of traditional meanings of well-known literary texts is devoutly to be desired. Its effect may be compared to the unsettling effect of evaluative criticism, but the deconstructive emphasis is so determinedly focused on the reappraisal of words and phrases in literary texts as to add a missing dimension to the reappraisal of the social and literary environment already described.

The remarkable impact of deconstruction in America is a direct consequence of the long pre-eminence of the New Criticism. The New Critical concentration on autonomous texts and neglect of their particular social environments took for granted the existence of an abstract environment in which it made sense to believe in absolute and permanent values. In doing so it did only what most of the intellectual world of its time did, inheriting its sense of metaphysical security from Kantian idealism and accepting that the unreliable nature of sense perception of phenomena was amply compensated for by the existence of an unobservable but deducible transcendent reality. Like so many inherited beliefs, this state of mind must have seemed to be merely common sense, and it coexisted comfortably with traditional religious faith.

The reliance of New Criticism on a metaphysical reality was neither deliberate nor wholly conscious, and it has come to matter only because of New Criticism's conscious and deliberate avoidance of physical reality. Evaluative criticism complained of this avoidance, but the crucial tactic of Jacques Derrida, the central theorist of deconstruction, has been to call into question the existence of a metaphysical reality and to leave the New Criticism in danger of having no reality to refer to at all.

Metaphysics, like linguistics, usually seems remote from literary criticism, but our practical thought and the language in which we conduct it generally take for granted a shared set of metaphysical assumptions. We have no difficulty in sensing the difference between our shared metaphysical assumptions and those of the Homeric world when we read of the personal intrusion of passionate gods and goddesses into human affairs. We are often made uneasy by the drama of the Renaissance with its acceptance of political authority, social hierarchy, and related codes of honour, and, although it is usual to regard our unease as a symptom of our progress in democracy, emphasis on our progress in democracy itself arguably depends upon increased scepticism about matters such as the existence of life after death and even of God. Derrida's intervention in literary criticism draws our attention to just such speculation, noting the precedents of Nietzsche and Heidegger:

> the Nietzschean critique of metaphysics, the critique of the concepts of being and truth, for which were substituted the concepts of play, interpretation, and sign (sign without truth present) . . . and, more radically, the Heideggerian destruction of metaphysics, of onto-theology, of the determination of being as presence.[46]

The general concepts of Nietzsche and Heidegger were already familiar, even to literary critics, but Derrida's application of them made apparent a practical consequence that seems to have been overlooked. If, as the arguments of these philosophers suggested, metaphysical reality was an illusion, it could not be regarded as a fixed point of reference against which our imperfectly perceived physical reality could be considered. Derrida makes the point positively in terms of its linguistic significance: 'The absence of the transcendental signified extends the domain and the interplay of signification *ad infinitum*.'[47] To put the matter in another way, if the meaning of statements is arrived at by juxtaposing them with reality and reality is unfixed and indeterminate, the meaning may be sought for indefinitely.

The practical application of deconstruction has been very various. Symptoms of it are to be found in criticism that might be more usually regarded as structuralist, such as Roland Barthes's *S/Z*, in which we are told that 'To interpret a text is not to give it a . . . meaning, but on the contrary to appreciate what *plural* constitutes it', and that 'the goal of the literary work . . . is to make the reader no longer a consumer, but a producer of the text.'[48] One of its characteristic strategies, the isolation of inconsistencies or internal contradictions in texts, has been employed for quite different purposes by Stanley Fish in his reflections on disputed cruxes in Milton's sonnets.[49] These approaches fulfil the deconstructive requirement that the critic attend to 'differences' within rather than between texts and proceed 'by the careful teasing out of warring forces of signification within the text itself'.[50] The apparent lack of an external inhibition has encouraged many critics to give their imaginations free play and in what seems to be a state of mutually supportive exhilaration to achieve new levels of critical invention and analytical subtlety.

In so far as literary criticism is a technique of interpretation, the prospect of being able to pursue it without the limitations of probability or verification may be superficially attractive, but the corollary of this extreme position seems to be that literary criticism is useless. We are left with criticism for criticism's sake. This development, however, follows upon the dissolution of metaphysical reality only if criticism insists, as the New Criticism did, on ignoring the connection between texts and physical reality. As soon as one restores the necessary part played by the social and literary environments in determining the meaning of texts, the Derridean challenge becomes more productive. Part of the challenge to historical criticism is to winnow the very real wheat from the unavoidable chaff by testing the results against what we know of the displaced environments. But historical critics who have the patience to make allowance for deconstruction's misses for the sake of its hits are likely to find also that their analytical tools are sharpened by keeping company with it.

V

In considering the relationship of historical criticism to the alternative modes from the perspective of the would-be historical critic, we should not forget that it is a mutual one. If the alternative modes have implications for the conduct of historical criticism, historical criticism has implications for the conduct of the alternative modes. These have been touched on from time to time along the way, but it may be useful briefly to gather their main features together for the consideration of critics whose approach to literature is not primarily historical.

The aim of historical criticism has been formulated as being the attempt to read past works of literature as they were read when they were new. It has been argued that various extraliterary matters have to be taken into account in making such an attempt and that certain imaginative constraints are placed upon the historical critic. These are part of the method by which original historical criticism is practised. It has also been maintained that historical criticism is a means to an end and not normally an end in itself. The end to which it is a means is the provision of reliable original meanings of texts for criticism of all kinds to work with; it is in turn an end to which textual criticism is a means.

Students of editorial theory will be familiar with the efforts made in scholarly editing, especially in the past sixty years, to ensure that the texts to which criticism is applied should be as close, word for word, to their original state as possible. Textual critics have made the case for the advantage of a sound and accurate text, and, while it cannot yet be said that sound and accurate texts are available for most of the major literary works of the past, there has been an enormous improvement in this regard, and the principle of being concerned about reliable texts and preferring them is generally conceded even by those who play no part in their preparation and who have little sympathy for the aims and methods of traditional textual criticism.

A literally accurate text is a vital first step in the critical process, but it is only a first step. Roland Barthes's concession to it suggests its limitations. 'Nobody', he says, 'has ever denied or will ever deny that the language of the text has a literal meaning, of which philology will, if necessary, inform us; what we need to know is whether or not one has the right to read in this literal language other meanings which do not contradict it.'[51] As Barthes knew perfectly well, we do not limit our sense of the meaning of modern works by recourse to dictionaries, and to read past works of literature in such a way could only be justified as an elementary academic exercise. An etymological dictionary might alert us to some changes in the meanings of words, but to be dependent on it as a reader is to miss the experience of reading for oneself. As I have argued in the first two chapters, the original meaning of a text, even of a literally accurate text, cannot be arrived at without a knowledge of the original environment of the text. The discrepancy between our capacity to recover the literal accuracy of a text and our capacity to recover the requisite knowledge of a past environment is so great that we may be reluctant to think that the meaning of the text depends upon a combination of the two. But, discouraging though it may seem to those who are used to the refined certainties or near-certainties of textual scholarship to be told that their results need to be combined with so uncertain or largely speculative an entity as a reconstructed displaced environment, there does not seem to be any other way of arriving at original meaning.

Together, textual criticism and historical criticism provide the raw materials of literature that other forms of criticism depend upon. They differ from one another in one important respect: while a satisfactory text arrived at by textual criticism may stand the test of time and remain fixed thereafter, the displaced environment recovered by historical criticism is in constant need of refurbishing because it is necessarily defined in terms of the modern environment. It may be added that the displaced environment is so imperfect by comparison with the 'definitive' text that in practical terms it seems that our information about it will be subject to improvement indefinitely. As a consequence, while a literary critic may acquire a sound text and feel able to rely on it thereafter, the reconstruction of the displaced environment without which the sound text will not render up its original meaning is subject to continuing change and improvement and can only be known by paying attention to the results of historical criticism.

It is usually at this point that impatience begins to be expressed. The attitude of mind of the historical critic is often felt to be uncongenial (alienation of the present is a corollary of the effort to approach the past), and historical criticism is still such an ill-organized enterprise that it is not easy to profit from its findings quickly or efficiently. It is understandable that critics who wish to concentrate their attention on the larger critical questions and who value intellectual consistency above all should be inclined to disregard the contributions of historical criticism as impractical antiquarianism. The belief that all criticism is ultimately dependent on the findings of historical criticism is an exceedingly uncomfortable one when one considers the level of adequacy achieved by historical criticism hitherto. None the less, however much we may sympathize with the fabled behaviour of the ostrich that buries its head in the sand on the approach of danger, we do not approve of it and would not wish to follow its example. The clear implication of the sorry state of historical criticism for criticism in general is that we can feel sure of the original meaning of hardly any of the works of literature of the past. If as critics we adopt the policy of assuming that they must have meant what they mean to us at first sight, we run risks that are amply documented and our commentaries, no matter how intelligent or sensitive we may be, are likely to have about as much bearing on the reality of the works they profess to discuss as the debates of the medieval controversialists about the number of angels that could dance on the head of a pin had on the reality of the world they lived in.

At the same time, the other modes of criticism obviously cannot wait for historical criticism to put its house in order. Imperfect though its understanding of the original meaning of past works may be, each generation will want to make of it what it can. Nor can every practising critic be expected to keep abreast of the findings of historical criticism on a broad front. But a tacit acknowledgement that critical results are understood to be subject to revision when and if more reliable information becomes available is less satisfactory than it seems to be at first. The saying that those who are ignorant of history are condemned to repeat its mistakes applies to historical criticism as well. As has been pointed out in earlier chapters, the canon of past works of literature and a set of presuppositions about what it means is part of every critic's education. Criticism that complacently disregards the advances of historical criticism is likely to accord its outmoded phases the status of common sense.[52] The critic's choice is between better historical criticism and worse historical criticism; criticism innocent of historical criticism is not an available option.

A viable compromise is not easy to point to, and can only be temporary in any case. But there seems to be some responsibility on the part of the exponent of historical criticism to suggest a practical expedient that will serve the alternative modes. There are two basic precautions by means of which the practising critic can make up for the deficiencies of historical criticism. The first is to read many examples of the kind of work being criticized and to take the trouble to read examples that fall outside the common range of readers – this precaution may be regarded as an absolute minimum. The second is to read many examples of works contemporary with the works one is criticizing, choosing various genres, and once again extending one's choice of texts to include examples that are usually neglected. Each of these precautions acts as a salutary check to the inadequate presuppositions about meaning that typically afflict the critic who does not make an active practice of historical criticism, and it will be found that by taking them in a generous spirit critics will often find themselves in advance of traditional historical criticism rather than behind it. A third precaution – consultation of current historical criticism of the works one is criticizing – is perhaps merely a way of seeming 'respectable', but it can provide one with access to the results of a more systematic and thoroughgoing version of the first two than anyone but a historical critic has time for.

NOTES

INTRODUCTION

1 A.S.P. Woodhouse, 'The historical criticism of Milton', *PMLA*, 66 (1951), p. 1,034, and Cleanth Brooks, 'Milton and critical re-estimates', *PMLA*, 66 (1951), p. 1,045. For a related presentation of the dichotomy as one between criticism and 'scholarship', see Lionel Trilling, *The Liberal Imagination* (New York, 1957), pp. 176–91.
2 This distinction is anticipated by R.S. Crane in his discussion of 'approaches' in criticism. See 'On hypothesis in "historical criticism"', in his *The Idea of the Humanities* (Chicago and London, 1967), II, pp. 247–8.
3 For an exposition of this distinction (derived ultimately from Frege), see E.D. Hirsch, Jr, *Validity in Interpretation* (New Haven and London, 1967), pp. 62–7.
4 A.S.P. Woodhouse includes the establishing of reliable texts as part of what he calls historical criticism (pp. 1,033–4). The alliance of the two enterprises is traditional.
5 See, for example, Lee Patterson, *Negotiating the Past: The Historical Understanding of Medieval Literature* (Madison, 1987); Stephen Greenblatt, *Renaissance Self-Fashioning from More to Shakespeare* (Chicago and London, 1980); Jerome J. McGann, *The Beauty of Inflections: Literary Investigations in Historical Method and Theory* (Oxford, 1985); and Lawrence Buell, *New England Literary Culture from Revolution through Renaissance* (Cambridge, 1986).

1 TRIANGLES OF INTERPRETATION

1 Or at which its self-evident meaning is judged to be unsatisfactory. But the deliberate substitution of meanings at odds with self-evident meanings, though equally traditional, is perhaps better thought of as literary misinterpretation or, less pejoratively, literary adaptation (on which see pp. 59–61 below).
2 Having a different point of view may be a consequence of having

information that others lack, but that was acquired prior to the need to interpret the text.
3 E.D. Hirsch, Jr, *Validity in Interpretation* (New Haven and London, 1967), pp. 1–4. Hirsch points out, quite rightly, that, although the term 'intentional fallacy' is widely used in this sense, value rather than meaning was what Wimsatt and Beardsley had in mind in the essay that popularized it; see pp. 11–12.
4 Hirsch, op. cit., pp. 5–6. In practice Hirsch is less absolute, allowing, usefully, the identification of genre as a further criterion of meaning; see especially pp. 68 ff. Fredric Jameson has suggested that this is 'the most interesting idea in the book' ('Metacommentary', *PMLA*, 86 (1971), p. 18).
5 For a historical summary of the fortunes of this line of theological defence, see Leslie Stephen, *History of English Thought in the Eighteenth Century* (London, 1876), chapter 9. Controversy over the extent to which the text of the Bible was by itself adequate evidence of God's intentions was its literary counterpart.
6 The implications of the god–author analogy for semantic autonomists are recognized in Roland Barthes, 'The death of the author', in *Image–Music–Text: Roland Barthes*, ed. Stephen Heath (London, 1977). For explicit dismissal of Hirsch's absolutism as politically reactionary, see Terry Eagleton, *Literary Theory: An Introduction* (Oxford, 1983), pp. 69–70. For an example of the complicated manoeuvring needed for even a sympathetic development of Hirsch's position, see P.D. Juhl, *Interpretation: An Essay in the Philosophy of Literary Criticism* (Princeton, 1980), especially pp. 12–32 and 37–9.
7 Something of the complexity of experience available to the individual reader is caught by Norman Holland in 'Re-covering "The Purloined Letter": reading as a personal transaction', in Susan R. Suleiman and Inge Crosman (eds), *The Reader and the Text: Essays on Audience and Interpretation* (Princeton, 1980), pp. 350–70; for the various experiences of different if ingenuous readers, see Norman Holland, *5 Readers Reading* (New Haven, 1975), and I.A. Richards's 'protocols' in *Practical Criticism* (London, 1929).
8 For an alternative but not incompatible analysis of these points of view as forms of linguistic theory, see the distinction developed between 'surrogationalism' and 'instrumentalism' in Roy Harris, *The Language-Makers* (London, 1980).
9 On the whole continental Europe seems to be of the 'French' persuasion and so are literary critics in America who specialize in the language and literature of continental Europe. This division of critics is obviously a crude one and should be used with caution. It provides a helpful organizing principle, e.g., in Toril Moi, *Sexual/Textual Politics: Feminist Literary Theory* (London and New York, 1985); for Moi's explanation, see p. xiv.
10 John Locke, *Essay Concerning Human Understanding*, book III, chapter 1, section 1. Descartes makes the possession of language one of the crucial symptoms of the possession of reason and one that divides human beings

from animals. (See René Descartes, *Discourse on Method*, part V, sections 58–9.)

11 Noam Chomsky, *Cartesian Linguistics: A Chapter in the History of Rationalist Thought* (New York and London, 1966), p. 17. Hans Aarsleff has demolished Chomsky's historical reconstructions in this book (see *From Locke to Saussure: Essays on the Study of Language and Intellectual History* (Minneapolis, 1982), pp. 101–19), but his strictures do not affect the reality of the philosophical distinctions that Chomsky was trying to illustrate.

12 For an analysis of the emergence of the 'expressive' theory, see M.H. Abrams, *The Mirror and the Lamp: Romantic Theory and the Critical Tradition* (1953; repr. New York, 1958), pp. 3, 21–6, and 28–9.

13 For a detailed account of the philological tradition, see Aarsleff, op. cit. See also his *The Study of Language in England, 1780–1860* (Princeton, 1967).

14 For a succinct summary of Saussure's theory, see Jonathan Culler, *Ferdinand de Saussure*, 2nd edn (Ithaca, 1986), pp. 27–64. For Saussure's relationship to the philological tradition, see Aarsleff, *From Locke to Saussure*.

15 For arguments in favour of the dominance of language over environment see, e.g., Benjamin Lee Whorf, *Language, Thought and Reality*, ed. John B. Carroll (1956; repr. Cambridge, Mass., 1964).

16 Parents' common habit of keeping alive the errors of small children or of talking to them in 'baby language' is a temporary exception.

17 The term 'utterance' is used here to mean not only what may be said but what may be conveyed by gesture, grimace, etc.

18 Cf. Roman Jakobson's analysis of message of addresser to addressee in which context, code, and contact are necessary elements: 'Linguistics and poetics', in *Style in Language*, ed. T. Sebeok (Cambridge, Mass., 1960), p. 353.

19 Or in the third instance at the conclusion that the utterance has no meaning as an utterance. The utterance might have 'significance', however, as evidence of the speaker's madness.

20 One can, of course, conceive of a statement that is ambiguous in both ways at once, but for the sake of explanation one ambiguity at a time seems sufficient and the method of clarification will still hold.

What a speaker means by a statement and what a speaker thinks his statement means are different questions. If a speaker absent-mindedly murmurs to himself, 'O for the wings of a dove', and is then asked by someone who overhears him, 'What do you mean?', he may, being made conscious of what he has murmured, say, 'I was thinking of that beautiful song' or 'I was wishing that I was far away from here', in each case providing the environment that the hearer lacked and making a conventional link between environment (his thought of the song, his wish to be far away) and language possible for the hearer. If, on the other hand, he declares that he was dreaming of tripe and onions, his hearer will be justified in thinking that, whatever the speaker meant by the words he said, the words he said did not mean what he meant. For a glimpse of the complications of trying to define a speaker's meaning (as

distinguished from the meaning of a speaker's statement), see Max Black, 'Meaning and intention: an examination of Grice's views', *New Literary History*, 4 (1973), pp. 257–79, and its useful bibliographical footnote (p. 257). For another viewpoint of the separation of such arguments from the topic at hand, interesting though they are in a slightly different context, see E.D. Hirsch, Jr, *The Aims of Interpretation* (Chicago and London, 1976), pp. 53–5. As Olsen has observed, 'If one does not want to accept the consequences of a general theory of meaning for authorial intention, one will have to revise the concept of literary meaning and deny any close parallel between that concept and linguistic meaning' (p. 32).
21 The case for the analogy is made systematically in Mary Louise Pratt, *Toward a Speech Act Theory of Literary Discourse* (Bloomington and London, 1977).
22 Cf. Jacques Derrida's strategic objection to the analogy, in *Margins of Philosophy*, trans. Alan Bass (Brighton, 1982), p. 329.
23 For a clear discussion of 'aspects of *vraisemblance*', which is related to what follows, see Jonathan Culler, *Structuralist Poetics: Structuralism, Linguistics and the Study of Literature* (London, Melbourne, and Henley, 1975), pp. 140–60.
24 Not, of course, that these were written as children's stories, but that they are used as if they were.
25 The extract is from Daisy Ashford, *The Young Visiters* (1919; repr. London, 1970), p. 37 (spelling corrected).
26 Olsen offers a useful model by pointing to 'a *community* of authors and readers' (p. 81), suggesting the analogy of games of chess (inexhaustibly various within certain agreed-upon conventions – pp. 22–3) and referring to a common institutional framework for literary works (pp. 81–3). These parallels are a needed corrective to exaggerated notions of authorial freedom of choice; to it must be added the acknowledgement that literary rules, unlike the rules of chess or of institutions, are not wholly defined, or wholly known, or inhospitable to innovation. Cf. H.P. Grice's consideration of the 'cooperative principle' in his 'Logic and conversation', *Syntax and Semantics*, 3 (1975), pp. 45–50.
27 Cf. Jerome J. McGann's dissatisfaction with the assumption in *A Critique of Modern Textual Criticism* (Chicago, 1983), p. 8.
28 The account given in Frank Lentricchia's *After the New Criticism* (Chicago, 1980), pp. 257–80, of E.D. Hirsch, Jr's advocacy of determinate meaning represents it as an anti-Romantic aberration. From a modern perspective it may seem to be, but a longer historical view suggests that modern assumptions are the aberration rather than Hirsch's.
29 For a measured sense of the relationship of life to literary convention in the *Confessions*, see Peter Brown, *Augustine of Hippo: A Biography* (London, 1967), pp. 158–81.
30 Emphasis on art as craft, carried to the opposite extreme, led the Russian formalist critic Osip Brik to assert that if Pushkin had not written *Eugene Onegin* someone else would have; see Peter Steiner, *Russian Formalism: A Metapoetics* (Ithaca, 1984), pp. 64–5. This point of

view and the analogy that he offered (Columbus discovering America) are not very satisfactory, but they point by their extravagance to an over-emphasis elsewhere on the idea of art as a form of self-expression.
31 An interest in Milton's psyche might be served by such a question – that is, it belongs to the domain of one kind of biographer. An interest in the process of composition might also benefit.

2 DISPLACED ENVIRONMENTS

1 A point made generally in E.H. Gombrich, *Art and Illusion* (London, 1960), and in a more particular way in *The Image and the Eye: Further Studies in the Psychology of Pictorial Representation* (Ithaca, 1982).
2 Cf. Stanley Fish's insistence on the kinetic element in reading, in *Is There a Text in This Class?* (Cambridge, Mass., and London, 1980), pp. 43–4.
3 For comment on the hazards incurred by ahistorical readers of philosophy, see D.W. Robertson, Jr, 'Some observations on method in literary studies', in Ralph Cohen (ed.), *New Directions in Literary History* (Baltimore, 1974), pp. 68–9. For an effective if fictional example, see the interpretation of the legend of St Eustace in Russell Hoban's novel *Riddley Walker* (London, 1980), pp. 118 ff.
4 Cf. the discussion of the modern failure to appreciate the force of the death of little Eva in *Uncle Tom's Cabin* in Jane P. Tompkins's 'Sentimental power: *Uncle Tom's Cabin* and the politics of literary history', in *The New Feminist Criticism: Essays on Women, Literature and Theory* (New York, 1985), pp. 85 ff.
5 For an account of the newness of the historical novel in Scott's time, see Georg Lukács, *The Historical Novel*, trans. Hannah and Stanley Mitchell (London, 1962), pp. 19–30.
6 The point is perhaps more familiar to students of Shakespeare who turn to North's Plutarch rather than to ancient Rome for such details of the past as his Roman plays contain, and fix their attention chiefly on Elizabethan England when they wish to understand what the plays originally meant.
7 *Lovers' Vows* had forty-two performances at Covent Garden in the 1798–9 season – far more than any other play. The fourth edition appeared in 1804.
8 Tate's version of Shakespeare's play held the stage from 1680 until 1823, when Shakespeare's ending was restored by Edmund Kean.
9 Joseph Anthony Wittreich, Jr, collects a very substantial representation of the new interpretation in *The Romantics on Milton* (Cleveland and London, 1970) and comments helpfully on its significance in his 'Introduction'.
10 D.W. Robertson, Jr, provides the conventional objection in 'Some observations on method in literary studies', pp. 71–3.
11 See *Ovid moralisé*, ed. C. de Boer, in *Verhandelingen der Koninklijke Akademie van Wetenschappen te Amsterdam: Afdeeling Letterkunde*, vols XV, XXI, XXX, XXXVII, XLIII–XLIV (Amsterdam, 1915–38), book I, lines 3,065–260; book II, lines 689–730; and book III, lines 604–69.

12 It might have been argued that God's foreknowledge embraced pagan literature as well, but this view does not seem to have been suggested.
13 For a discussion of the place of a canon of significant art and of its validity in spite of such mistakes and of changes of fashion, see Ernst Gombrich, *Ideals and Idols: Essays on Values in History and Art* (Oxford, 1979).
14 For a full presentation of the Shakespearian originals, see Geoffrey Bullough, *Narrative and Dramatic Sources of Shakespeare*, 8 vols (London and New York, 1957–75).
15 The term 'aesthetically' is used here in its most comprehensive sense – including 'morally satisfying'.
16 In the case of a work that has achieved fame in an inaccurate form – say, Bach's keyboard music played on a piano instead of a harpsichord – the 'original effect' may be that of the inaccurate form.
17 See Roland Barthes, *On Racine*, trans. Richard Howard (New York, 1983), and Raymond Picard, *Nouvelle critique ou nouvelle imposture* (Paris, 1965).

3 KNOWLEDGES OF THE PAST

1 For an acknowledgement of the imperfection of such attempts at recovery and an exploration, nevertheless, of their importance, see, for example, Virginia Woolf, 'On not knowing Greek', *Collected Essays* (London, 1966), I, pp. 1–13.
2 Cf. Michael Oakeshott's distinction between what he calls the 'practical past' and the 'recorded past' for the similar residue of popular knowledge that faces the historian, in *On History and Other Essays* (Oxford, 1983), pp. 16–19, 34–44, and 30–3.
3 My discussion here is influenced by Arthur C. Danto, *Narrative and Knowledge* (New York, 1985). His argument, in turn, is anticipated for my purposes in important respects by Marc Bloch, *The Historian's Craft*, trans. Peter Putnam (New York, 1953), chapter 2, which discusses the capacities and limitations of historical knowledge with informal authority.
4 This tripartite division of knowledge is traditional and may be seen, for example, in Bertrand Russell, *Our Knowledge of the External World* (1914; repr. London, 1952), p. 74, where Russell speaks of 'our own personal sensible acquaintance', 'testimony', and 'science'.
5 To which might be added such internal phenomena as headaches, toothaches, etc.
6 Instinct, which we also appear to share, seems to be largely independent of our environment and is less likely to be affected by its displacement. It may be an important link with our predecessors (see, for example, the role of direct experience that is shared or typical – p. 72 below), but it still awaits historical investigation.
7 A distinction might be made between our direct observation of, say, television news and our direct observation of an event, but for the most

part and unless we have particular reason to be suspicious we seem to accept what is shown as being what is, or was, there.
8 Certain qualifications of this statement must be allowed. A witness of a crime can sometimes be induced to recall details that seemed to be insignificant at the time when it was committed, but this capacity is short-lived. Further exceptions may be made for memory induced by hypnosis, by brain surgery, or even in the course of dreams. In these circumstances we may perhaps be said to remember what we had forgotten.
9 Previous knowledge may consist of an interrelated whole that is constantly refreshed by experiences that modify or confirm it.
10 Yellow vision is apparently a rare symptom of jaundice.
11 In his discussion of Dilthey's philosophy of history, Hans Georg Gadamer seems to overlook this possibility when he states that 'the historical world . . . is always a world that is constituted and formed by the human mind': *Truth and Method* (New York, 1975), p. 196.
12 In another sense history too may be studied as a means to an end – moral improvement, say, or greater wisdom; in that sense the historical critic may also hope to become wiser by being better informed.
13 Following the distinction made by Saussure between 'synchronic' and 'diachronic' study of language – between 'study of the linguistic system in a particular state, without reference to time' and 'study of its evolution in time' (Jonathan Culler, *Ferdinand de Saussure*, 2nd edn (Ithaca, 1986), p. 45) – this is called 'synchronic history', as opposed to 'diachronic history'. For resistance to it from more traditional historians, see, for example, G.R. Elton, *The Practice of History* (1967; repr. London, 1984), p. 167: 'There is a clear and admirable sense of life, but how those lives passed through history is much less clear.'
14 For doubts about the untaintedness of such 'primary sources', see Peter Munz, *The Shapes of Time: A New Look at the Philosophy of History* (Middletown, 1977), pp. 173–203.
15 The term 'documents' here should be regarded as including surviving physical evidence of any kind, and the term 'events' as including literary events.

The emergence of what is being termed the 'New Historicism' (see, for example, the essays in Stephen Greenblatt (ed.), *The Power of Forms in the English Renaissance* (Norman, 1982)) reveals the need for a further distinction by seeming to overlook it. The New Historicism shows a promising interest in the relationship between literature and its social environment by examining the documentary evidence of that environment (charters, proclamations, etc.) as if it was of a piece with literature, but it tends to ignore the difference between fact and fiction. In so far as the original readers were unaware of the difference, this procedure appears to satisfy the requirements of historical criticism, but the historical critic will wish to know when the texts were perceived as having a factual basis. Modern analogies would be the difference in our experience on the one hand of novels such as D.M. Thomas's *The White Hotel*, with its scenes from Babi Yar, or Primo Levi's *If Not Now, When?*, with its

unremitting attention to the Holocaust, and on the other hand of novels such as Burgess's *A Clockwork Orange*. It is difficult to know quite where or how to draw the line between the presentation of fact in fiction and the presentation of 'sheer' fiction, but as readers we seem to react differently to the two modes.
16 Significant events for the historian need not be so spectacular as the Battle of Waterloo, and indeed much modern history patiently examines a multitude of seemingly insignificant events, but usually in the hope of perceiving a significant trend or of generalizing about the nature of a recurrent kind of event.
17 A point made by René Wellek in his essay 'Literary theory, criticism, and history', in his *Concepts of Criticism*, ed. Stephen J. Nichols, Jr (New Haven and London, 1963), p. 15.
18 The existence of dramatic poems or closet dramas acknowledges the norm while claiming to be excepted from it. For a detailed theoretical account of the difference between a play read and a play seen in performance, see Roman Ingarden, *The Literary Work of Art: An Investigation on the Borderlines of Ontology, Logic, and Theory of Literature*, trans. George G. Grabowicz (Evanston, 1973), pp. 317–29.
19 For an appreciative perception of the presence of the past, see Patrick Wright, *On Living in an Old Country: The National Past in Contemporary Britain* (London, 1985); for an awareness of the hazards of assuming its presence too readily, see Richard Holmes, *Footsteps of a Romantic Biographer* (1985; repr. Harmondsworth, 1986), pp. 66–9.
20 The treatment of such materials in Richard Hoggart's *The Uses of Literacy: Aspects of Working-Class Life with Special Reference to Publications and Entertainments* (London, 1957) has already begun to be a useful reminder of a vanished environment.
21 A better historian's equivalent might be the present. See, for example, Marc Bloch's remark that 'it is always by borrowing from our daily experiences and by shading them, where necessary, with new tints that we derive the elements which help us to restore the past' (op. cit., p. 44).

4 STRATEGIES

1 For criticism of the works of a group of related writers that provides a promising variant on the single-author approach, preserving the valuable focus without limiting it to one person's point of view, see S.P. Rosenbaum's *Victorian Bloomsbury: The Early Literary History of the Bloomsbury Group* (New York, 1987).
2 Many plays that were performed but not published have been lost, however, and the acting companies were often reluctant to publish and thereby make texts available to rival companies.
3 See, for example, the discussion in Jerome J. McGann, *A Critique of Modern Textual Criticism* (Chicago and London, 1983), pp. 19–22.
4 For a comparison of Aristotle's approach in *The Poetics* to that of a biologist, see Northrop Frye, *Anatomy of Criticism*, p. 14; the Linnaean

precedent is suggested in Vladimir Propp, *Morphology of the Folktale*, trans. Louis A. Wagner (Austin and London, 1970), p. 11.

5 J.H. Hexter considers the similar implications for historians of 'team projects' and of Braudel's readiness to see the end of 'l'histoire artisanal'; see *On Historians* (Cambridge, Mass., 1979), pp. 90–3.

6 The imperfections of microforms should be acknowledged. They are more tiring to read than books; they are occasionally badly photographed, being out of focus or missing pages; it is difficult to find pages that are not adjacent to the page one is reading. It is to be hoped that these deficiencies will become rarer as the form becomes more familiar.

7 Georg Christoph Lichtenberg's collection is available as *Lichtenberg's Commentaries on Hogarth's Engravings*, trans. Innes and Gustav Herdan (London, 1966).

8 He lived in England in 1769 and 1774 and published an account of his stay in *Briefe aus England* (1776–8). Most of Hogarth's pictures were produced in the 1730s and 1740s.

9 This observation holds true of art galleries too where pictures thought to be artistically less interesting are often kept in storage because of lack of space.

10 Two of the best known of these catalogues are *The Index of Christian Art* at Princeton University – an iconographic index of over 700,000 cards and 200,000 photographs – and the less specialized Photographic Collection of the Warburg Institute in the University of London.

11 For a lively account of this progress in England, see Richard Altick, *The Shows of London* (Cambridge, Mass., and London, 1978).

12 Now housed on the top two floors of the Science Museum in South Kensington. At the other end of the scale are amateur collections of objects such as the one of over 2 million items used in the region of Nottinghamshire between 1800 and 1950 (see *The Times*, 19 August 1987, p. 1), which through lack of public appreciation are in danger of being broken up.

13 After the journal *Annales d'histoire économique et sociale*, founded in 1929.

14 Lucien Febvre's *Life in Renaissance France*, ed. and trans. Marian Rothstein (Cambridge, Mass., 1977), is a good example of such imaginings.

15 For an accessible and intelligent account of the origin of what has come to be called 'method acting', see Eric Bentley, *The Theory of the Modern Stage* (Harmondsworth, 1968), pp. 219–74.

16 From a bibliographical point of view no two copies are 'identical', but from the point of view of past public acquaintance with them the differences are usually negligible.

17 Publishers' advertisements have to be treated with caution because books are sometimes announced but not actually published.

18 It may be objected that later ages will have been more likely to preserve the works they have cared about, but their preference will also be confusingly reflected in the existence of multiple copies and modern reprints. Even 'bad' books are not usually destroyed by their owners,

and officially suppressed books are often carefully preserved by dissident collectors.
19 It also indexes by place of publication, making exhaustive investigation of publication in provincial centres much easier than before.
20 For a detailed account of what is already available, see *The Eighteenth Century Short Title Catalogue*, ed. R.C. Alston and M.J. Crump (London, 1983), 'Introduction'; union short-title catalogues of the nineteenth century have begun to appear, Series I (1801–14) being complete. For comment on some of the opportunities as well as accompanying problems, see M. Crump and M. Harris, *Searching the Eighteenth Century* (London, 1983).
21 This estimate is arrived at by multiplying the number of titles shown on one frame of the microfiche (an average of 55) by the number of frames required to record the year's holdings (31½).
22 This estimate is arrived at by multiplying the 1775 figure by 20, a method that allows in a rough and ready way for the slight increase in numbers of books published annually during the period by choosing the middle date as a norm.
23 One of the most valuable aspects of Northrop Frye's *Anatomy of Criticism* has been its systematic definition of this tradition.
24 Certain obvious exceptions – books related to institutions such as the church, the telephone system, etc. – have an enduring 'popularity' that does not depend on reading them through.
25 See Roland W. Clark, *Einstein: The Life and Times* (London, Sydney, Auckland, and Toronto, 1971), pp. 223–8.

5 THE RELATIONSHIP OF HISTORICAL CRITICISM TO SOME ALTERNATIVE MODES

1 Adopting innovative critical procedures for purposes not foreseen by the original innovators is too traditional to require apology. For interesting recent examples of such adoptions, see Michael Ryan, *Marxism and Deconstruction* (Baltimore, 1982).
2 For a pertinent discussion of the origin of the historical term 'Middle Ages' and its concomitant, the 'Renaissance', see Marc Bloch, *The Historian's Craft*, trans. Peter Putnam (New York, 1953), pp. 178–81.
3 These figures are roughly arrived at, especially the first, the date of the earliest Old English writings being in dispute.
4 For the place of etymology in this adoption, see John Cross, *The Rise and Fall of the English Man of Letters* (London, 1969), p. 169.
5 For misgivings about this transfer, see Jerome J. McGann, *A Critique of Modern Textual Criticism* (Chicago and London, 1983), pp. 37 ff.
6 Donald Greene, *The Age of Exuberance: Backgrounds to Eighteenth-Century English Literature* (New York, 1970). For a more detailed consideration of the shortcomings of literary history and a speculative explanation of the ways in which they have developed, see Hans Robert Jauss, *Toward an Aesthetics of Reception*, trans. Timothy Bahti (Minneapolis, 1982), pp. 3–18.

A similar argument has been conducted over the appositeness of 'Augustan' as a description of early eighteenth-century satire. See, for instance, Howard D. Weinbrot, *Augustus Caesar in 'Augustan' England: The Decline of a Classical Norm* (Princeton and Guildford, 1978); Howard Erskine-Hill, *The Augustan Idea in English Literature* (London, 1983); and Claude Rawson, *Order from Confusion Sprung* (London, Boston, and Sydney, 1985), pp. 242–58.

7 René Wellek, 'Romanticism re-examined', in Northrop Frye (ed.), *Romanticism Reconsidered* (New York and London, 1963), p. 107.

8 Cf. Jerome J. McGann, *The Romantic Ideology: A Critical Investigation* (Chicago and London, 1983), p. 18: 'the subsequent critical literature on Romanticism eloquently testifies to the triumph of his general position.'

9 John Locke, *An Essay Concerning Human Understanding*, book II, chapter 11, section 2: 'wit, lying most in the assemblage of ideas, and putting these together with quickness and variety wherein can be found any resemblance or congruity, thereby to make up pleasant pictures and agreeable visions in the fancy; judgment, on the contrary, lies quite on the other side, in separating carefully one from another ideas wherein can be found the least difference, thereby to avoid being misled by similitude and affinity to take one thing for another.' J.H. Hexter brings the distinction up to date by suggesting that people are either 'lumpers' or 'splitters'; see his *On Historians* (Cambridge, Mass., 1979), pp. 241–2.

10 For recent comment on this practice, see McGann, *The Romantic Ideology*, pp. 17–56. For doubts about bringing prior categorical expectations to poems, see George Whalley, 'Literary Romanticism', *Queen's Quarterly*, 72 (1965), pp. 232–52. A.D. Harvey's *English Poetry in a Changing Society, 1780–1825* (London, 1980) draws attention to the literature and literary milieu neglected by such expectations. The broader methodological implications of such differences of opinion are discussed by Karl R. Popper under the heading of 'Essentialism *versus* nominalism' in his *The Poverty of Historicism*, 2nd edn (London, 1960), pp. 26–34. In dismissing such concepts as 'the spirit of the age', however, Popper allows both that they may be useful correctives to the old-fashioned identification of the past with outstanding individuals and that they may indicate a genuine need for more study of what he calls the 'logic of situations' (see ibid., pp. 147–52).

11 A case for this use of objectivity is made in Northrop Frye, *Anatomy of Criticism*, pp. 17–29. Cf. the similar claim from the perspective of literary history in Hans Ulrich Gumbrecht, 'History of literature – fragment of a vanished totality', *New Literary History*, 16 (1984–5), pp. 471–2.

12 Terry Eagleton says of the criticism of Raymond Williams that it 'rests on a rare, courageously simple belief . . . that the deepest personal experience can be offered, without arrogance or appropriation, as socially "typical"': *Criticism and Ideology: A Study in Marxist Literary Theory* (London, 1976), p. 23. The belief itself, however, is not the determinant of the success of such criticism; it is either confirmed by its readers or not.

13 R.P. Bilan's chapter, 'The idea of criticism', in his *The Literary Criticism of*

F.R. Leavis (Cambridge, 1979), pp. 61–82, provides a sympathetic and lucid account of Leavis's intentions.
14 His most explicit statement on this issue occurs in *The Common Pursuit* (London, 1952), pp. 211–22.
15 See Matthew Arnold, 'The function of criticism at the present time', in *Essays in Criticism* (First Series); Arnold's recommendation was of course anticipated by Kant's account of the judgement of taste (*Critique of Judgment*, book I, part 1, section 13) in 1790, but continental innovations are often slow to be adopted in the English-speaking world.
16 Leavis was educated at the Perse School in Cambridge. For the difference between that environment and the environment of Cambridge University, see William Walsh, *F.R. Leavis* (Bloomington and London, 1980), pp. 9–12.
17 This formulation should not be understood too narrowly. For a sensible discussion of what it ought and ought not to mean, see Terry Eagleton, *Marxism and Literary Criticism* (London, 1976), pp. 9–16.
18 The five-volume *New Cambridge Bibliography of English Literature* (1969–77), large though it is, deliberately omits many 'minor authors' whose works were recorded in its five-volume predecessor, *The Cambridge Bibliography of English Literature* (1940–57); that bibliography in turn recorded only a small fraction of extant literature.
19 To whom may be added circulating libraries, public libraries, etc. This 'sociology of literature' is dismissed by Terry Eagleton as 'for the most part a suitably tamed, de-gutted version of Marxist criticism', and he adds that it is 'appropriate for Western consumption' (*Marxism and Literary Criticism*, p. 3). His own alternative is more challenging, offering the following 'major constituents of a Marxist theory of literature': (1) general mode of production, (2) literary mode of production, (3) general ideology, (4) authorial ideology, (5) aesthetic ideology, (6) text (see *Criticism and Ideology*, p. 44 and ff.). The emphasis on economic factors is apparent here, but the 'constituents' are rhetorical pointers to what one might like to know rather than elements that can be considered by those who are interested in them; as yet hardly anything is known about what he calls 'general mode of production' and literary mode of production'.
20 See, for example, Fredric Jameson, *The Political Unconscious: Narrative as a Socially Symbolic Act* (Ithaca, 1981). For reservations about the limiting effects of the motivating political bias, see Gerald Graff, 'The pseudo-politics of interpretation', *Critical Inquiry*, 9 (1983), pp. 597–610, and, from a more particularly historical perspective, Edward Pechter, 'The New Historicism and its discontents: politicizing Renaissance drama', *PMLA*, 102 (1987), pp. 292–303.
21 For the connection with Marxist criticism, see, for example, the recommendation of what Eagleton called 'sociology of literature' in Rosalind Coward, 'Are women's novels feminist novels?', in Elaine Showalter (ed.), *The New Feminist Criticism* (New York, 1985), p. 226; for an examination of the relationship with Marxist criticism, see Elaine Showalter, 'Toward a feminist poetics', in Showalter (ed.), *The New Feminist Criticism*, pp. 139–42. For an appreciative discussion of the

richness of the feminist approach as a demonstration of the existence of a point of view that for non-feminists is at once alien and familiar and therefore analogous to the historical perspective, see Jonathan Culler, *On Deconstruction: Theory and Criticism after Structuralism* (Ithaca, 1982), pp. 42–64.
22 Criticism of Canadian literature, Australian literature, etc., seems to be going through a related sequence of development.
23 The closeness of the criticism of American literature to the feminist approach surfaces interestingly as conflict between them, the nationalist definition of American literature having stressed those aspects of social experience in which America was unique – exploration, pioneering, conflict with nature and with native peoples – and de-emphasizing the common social ground – domestic life. See, for example, the protest against this accidentally man-centred perception of experience in Nina Baym, 'Melodramas of beset manhood: how theories of American fiction exclude women authors', in Showalter (ed.), op. cit., pp. 63–80. For reflections on the general implications of changing one's sense of the received body of literature, see John Guillory, 'Canonical and non-canonical: a critique of the current debate', *ELH*, 54 (1987), pp. 483–527.
24 See, for example, Showalter (ed.), op. cit., p. 36: 'Everything has to be done again'; p. 59: 'a revisionist reading of our entire literary inheritance'; p. 341: 'literary *history* remains a male preserve'.
25 For example, Jane Tompkins, 'Sentimental power: *Uncle Tom's Cabin* and the politics of literary history', in Showalter (ed.), op. cit., pp. 81–104.
26 See, for instance, Henry Nash Smith, 'The scribbling women and the cosmic success story', *Critical Inquiry*, 1 (1974–5), pp. 47–50, where the effect of popular American fiction on 'serious' novelists is considered.
27 Cf. the overlapping-circles formulation proposed by Edwin Ardener and cited in Showalter (ed.), op. cit., pp. 261–3.
28 The dismissal of the aims of historical criticism in Annette Kolodny, 'Dancing through the minefield', in Showalter (ed.), op. cit., pp. 152–3, is based on rejection of the authority of the author rather than on rejection of the displaced environment.
29 The rather hostile political explanation of the popularity of Frye's approach in Terry Eagleton's *Literary Theory: An Introduction* (Oxford, 1983), pp. 91–4, may contain some elements of truth, but it does not allow for the persuasiveness of success in the classroom. And W.K. Wimsatt's cogent objections to the particular system of classification employed by Frye (see his 'Northrop Frye: criticism as myth', in Murray Krieger (ed.), *Northrop Frye in Modern Criticism* (New York and London, 1966), pp. 75–107) may be allowed without essential damage to its usefulness as a challenging and even inspiring educational model.
30 See *The Bush Garden* (Toronto, 1971). Eagleton treats the emphasis on the literary environment and comparative neglect of the social environment in political terms (*Literary Theory*, pp. 92–4); again this perspective seems more applicable to Frye's reception than to Frye himself.

31 Frye's awareness of the need to account for all kinds of literature and to avoid leaving out the 'insignificant' is perfectly apparent – see, for example, *Anatomy*, pp. 19 and 20–4.
32 He explicitly acknowledges the fluctuations of literary fashion, however – see *Anatomy*, p. 25.
33 This assumption of timelessness is not explicit in *Anatomy* but seems to be taken for granted. It bears an interesting resemblance to the view of literature as a form of divine revelation that was expounded by James Harris in the eighteenth century under the name of 'divine philology' – see Robert Marsh, *Four Dialectical Theories of Poetry* (Chicago, 1965), pp. 159–70 – although the precedent Frye cites is T.S. Eliot's *The Function of Criticism*; see *Anatomy*, p. 18.
34 See Northrop Frye, *Fables of Identity: Studies in Poetic Mythology* (New York and Burlingame, 1963), pp. 107–8. Cf. the summation of discussion up to that time in J.H.P. Pafford's Arden edition of the play (London and Cambridge, Mass., 1963).
35 The comparison is commonplace; see, for example, David Lodge, *Working with Structuralism: Essays and Reviews on Nineteenth and Twentieth-Century Literature*, 2nd edn (London, Boston, and Henley, 1986), p. 18. There is some warrant for regarding psychological criticism too as being an anticipation of structuralism. If one believes psychological theory to be an objective account of reality (to be compared with anthropological and linguistic theory in this respect) then it seems reasonable to read literary works in the light of it (as do the Freudians Ernest Jones in *Hamlet and Oedipus* (New York, 1949) and Norman Holland in *The Dynamics of Literary Response* (New York, 1968)). The existence of competing psychological theories (most notably of Freud and Jung, but more recently of Lacan and Irigaray, to say nothing of those of Adler, Klein, etc., which have not yet had much of a literary following) suggests that the objectivity aimed at has not yet been attained. As structural models, however, they are useful in somewhat the same way as Frye's theory. (The affinities are touched on in Murray Krieger, *Theory of Criticism: A Tradition and its System* (Baltimore and London, 1976), pp. 150–1.)
36 For a clear introduction to the assumptions of structuralism and to its more significant critical applications, see Jonathan Culler, *Structuralist Poetics: Structuralism, Linguistics and the Study of Literature* (London, Melbourne, and Henley, 1975). For a succinct discussion of the various meanings of 'structuralism', see Jonathan Culler, *On Deconstruction*, pp. 18–22.
37 Or, as Lévi-Strauss puts it, they shift 'from the study of conscious phenomena to that of their unconscious infrastructure'; quoted in Culler, *Structuralist Poetics*, p. 28. Paul de Man identifies the consequent advantage to criticism when he observes that our attention to content competes with our awareness of form: 'the perception of the literary dimensions of language is largely obscured if one submits uncritically to the authority of reference' (*Allegories of Reading* (New Haven and London, 1979), p. 5).

38 See Claude Lévi-Strauss, *The Scope of Anthropology*, trans. Sherry Ortner Paul and Robert A. Paul (London, 1967), pp. 34–40.
39 See, for example, Umberto Eco's analysis of 'The myth of Superman', trans. Natalie Chilton, *Diacritics*, 2 (1972), pp. 14–22.
40 Roman Ingarden, *The Literary Work of Art: An Investigation on the Borderlines of Ontology, Logic, and Theory of Literature*, trans. George G. Grabowicz (Evanston, 1973), pp. 20–5, and especially p. 23.
41 ibid., p. 29.
42 Roman Ingarden, *The Cognition of the Literary Work of Art*, trans. Ruth Ann Crowley and Kenneth R. Olson (Evanston, 1973), pp. 50–2.
43 See Norman Holland, 'Re-covering "The Purloined Letter": a reading as a personal transaction', in Susan R. Suleiman and Inge Crosman (eds), *The Reader in the Text: Essays on Audience and Interpretation* (Princeton, 1980), p. 350.
44 Holland's early awareness of the likelihood that the passage of time may alter the way in which we read is apparent in his submission to D.W. Robertson, Jr's correction of his reading of 'The Wife of Bath's Tale' as non-medieval; see *The Dynamics of Literary Response*, pp. 22–5.
45 The scepticism about the 'historical approach' as a determinant of meaning expressed in Jonathan Culler's account of Derrida's views and practice seems to be based on his rejection of either author's original meaning or reader's 'creative experience' as determinants of meaning. But, as he admits, Derrida's attitude to history is ambivalent and perhaps the concept of reference to displaced environments would seem acceptable as the determinant of the kind of meaning; see *On Deconstruction*, pp. 128–32.
46 Jacques Derrida, 'Structure, sign, and play in the discourse of the human sciences', in Richard Macksey and Eugenio Donato (eds), *The Languages of Criticism and the Sciences of Man: The Structuralist Controversy* (Baltimore and London, 1970), p. 250.
47 ibid., p. 249.
48 Roland Barthes, *S/Z*, trans. Richard Miller (New York, 1974), pp. 5 and 4.
49 See Stanley Fish, 'Interpreting the *Variorum*', *Critical Inquiry*, 2 (1976), pp. 465–85.
50 Barbara Johnson, *The Critical Difference: Essays in the Contemporary Rhetoric of Reading* (Baltimore and London, 1980), p. 5.
51 Roland Barthes, *Criticism and Truth*, trans. Katrine Pilcher Keuneman (London, 1987), p. 39. M.H. Abrams sums up the consequence of such an attitude in his description of a procedure used by deconstructionist critics (specifically Derrida and J. Hillis Miller): 'Any word within a given text . . . can thus be claimed to signify any and all of the diverse things it has signified in the varied forms that the signifier has assumed through its recorded history; and not only in a particular language, such as English or French, but back through its etymology in Latin and Greek all the way to its postulated Indo-European root' ('The deconstructive angel', *Critical Inquiry*, 3 (1977), p. 433).

52 Historical criticism is like theoretical approaches in this respect. See, for example, Terry Eagleton, *Literary Theory: An Introduction* (Oxford, 1983), p. vii: 'J.M. Keynes once remarked that those economists who disliked theory, or claimed to get along better without it, were simply in the grip of an older theory. This is also true of literary students and critics.'

REFERENCES

The following works are those cited in the text by author and/or page number only:

Allen, Don Cameron, 'Foreword' to A.O. Lovejoy, *Essays in the History of Ideas*, pp. vii–ix, 1948; repr. New York, 1960.

Augustine, St, *On Christian Doctrine*, trans. D.W. Robertson, Jr, New York, 1958.

Brooks, Cleanth, 'Milton and critical re-estimates', *PMLA*, 66, 1951, pp. 1,045–54.

Collingwood, R.G., *The Idea of History*, Oxford, 1946.

Frye, Northrop, *Anatomy of Criticism: Four Essays*, Princeton, 1957.

Iser, Wolfgang, *The Implied Reader: Patterns of Communication in Prose Fiction from Bunyan to Beckett*, Baltimore and London, 1974.

Leavis, F.R., *Letters on Criticism*, ed. John Tasker, London, 1974.

Lovejoy, A.O., *Essays in the History of Ideas*, 1948; repr. New York, 1960.

Ogden, C.K., and Richards, I.A., *The Meaning of Meaning*, 1923; repr. London, 1985.

Olsen, Stein Haugom, *The End of Literary Theory*, Cambridge, 1987.

Robertson, D.W., Jr, 'Historical criticism', in Alan S. Downer (ed.), *English Institute Essays: 1950*, pp. 3–31, New York, 1951.

Taine, H., *Histoire de la littérature anglaise*, vol. I, 1871; repr. Paris, 1905.

Wellek, René, *Concepts of Criticism*, ed. Stephen G. Nichols, Jr, New Haven and London, 1963.

Welty, Eudora, *Critical Inquiry*, 1, 1974–5, pp. 219–21.

Woodhouse, A.S.P., 'The historical criticism of Milton', *PMLA*, 66, 1951, pp. 1,033–44.

INDEX

Aarsleff, Hans 154
Abrams, M. H. 154, 166
Academy, French 99
actes gratuites 144–5
acting: history of 76; method 108
acts, speech 21, 24; *see also* utterances
adaptations, dramatic 59, 60
Adler, Alfred 165
aestheticism 127
Allen, Don Cameron 106–7
Alston, R. C. 161
ambiguity 20, 32
Annales school 108–9
Ardener, Edwin 164
Aristotle 159
Arnold, Matthew 51, 127, 163
art: catalogues of 103–4; fine and applied distinguished 35; history of 103–4; survival of works of 37
Ashford, Daisy: *The Young Visiters* 155
Augustine, St: *The Confessions* 34; *De Doctrina Christiana* 57
Austen, Jane 38; *Mansfield Park* 49–50
author, authority of 11, 31–6
autonomy, semantic 9–10, 11
awareness, historical 5

Bach, J. S. 157
Bacon, Francis 92
Barthes, Roland 61, 146, 148, 153, 157, 166
Baym, Nina 164
Beardsley, Monroe 153
Beaumont and Fletcher 115
beliefs, public and private 82
Bentley, Eric 160
Bentley, G. E. 95–6

Beowulf 37–8
Bible 29, 85, 153
bibliographies 99–100
Bilan, R. P. 162–3
Bizet, Georges: *Carmen* 60–1
Black, Max 154–5
Blake, William 4, 51
Bloch, Marc 63, 108, 157, 159, 161
Book of Common Prayer 85
botany 98–9, 112
Bowers, Fredson 96, 120
Braudel, Fernand 108, 160
Brik, Osip 155
Brooks, Cleanth 2, 5, 152
Brooks, Peter: *Carmen* 60–1
Brown, Peter 155
Buell, Lawrence 152
Bullough, Geoffrey 157
Burgess, Anthony: *A Clockwork Orange* 159
Burke, Edmund: 'On Conciliation with the Colonies' 74–5
Byron, George Gordon, Lord, 93, 125: *Childe Harold's Pilgrimage* 51; *Don Juan* 51

canon: literary 50–2, 54, 128, 129–32, 135–6; Shakespeare's 115
catalogues, library 109–12
certainty, negative 78–9, 80, 82, 84–5
Cervantes, Miguel de 113
chain of being 82, 107
chairs, makers of 34–5
Chambers, E. K. 95–6
Chaucer, Geoffrey: *The Canterbury Tales* 50; 'The Nun's Priest's Tale' 103;

Chaucer, Geoffrey (*cont.*):
  Troilus and Criseyde 50; 'The Wife of Bath's Tale' 166
Chippendale, Thomas, the elder 35
Chomsky, Noam 154
Christie, Agatha: *The Murder of Roger Ackroyd* 28
Clare, John 4
Clark, R. W. 161
Coleridge, S. T. 37, 93–4
collator, Hinman 96
Collingwood, R. G. 86–7
Columbus 69, 156
communications 101
complex, Oedipus 55, 108
computers 111
concretization 140
Condillac, Etienne de 13
confessions 34
Cotton, Sir Robert 37
Coward, E. R. 163
Crane, R. S. 152
criterion, moral 10
criticism: archetypal 7, 134–7; English-speaking vs French-speaking 12–13; evaluative 7, 125–34, 138, 145; feminist 7, 55, 131–4, 163–4; historical: aims of 1, 3–4, 71–2, 77–8, 110, deficiencies of 2, 55, defined 1, 2, 3–5; history and 71–3; method of 3; new criticism and 2–3, 5; Marxist 7, 128–31, 133, 134, 163; nationalist 131–2, 164; new 2, 3, 5, 54, 134, 138, 139, 141, 145, 147; psychological 165; reader-response 7, 139–43; textual 148–9
Crump, M. J. 161
Culler, Jonathan 154, 155, 158, 164, 165, 166

Danto, A. C. 157
Darwinism, social 82, 107
deconstruction 7, 143–7
Defoe, Daniel 54; *Robinson Crusoe* 29, 87
deism 107
de Man, Paul 165
Derrida, Jacques 145–7, 155, 166
Descartes, René 19, 82, 153–4
Dickens, Charles 50, 93; *David Copperfield* 42–3; *The Old Curiosity Shop* 44, 142
dictionaries 99–100
Diderot: *Encyclopédie* 99
Dilthey, Wilhelm 158
disinterestedness 125–6, 127

documents 74–6
Donne, John: 'The Ecstasy' 53, 54
drama, Renaissance 95–7, 146
Dryden, John 50; *The State of Innocence* 75–6
dualism 19
Dyer, George 94

Eagleton, Terry 153, 162, 163, 164, 167
Eco, Umberto 166
economics, literary 130
Einstein, Albert 116
Eliot, George 132
Eliot, T. S. 4, 165; *Four Quartets* 4; 'The Love Song of J. Alfred Prufrock' 32
Elton, J. R. 158
encyclopaedias 99–100
enthymeme 21
environment 6, 23–6; ambiguous 20; defined 15, 23–4, 39; displaced 6, 37–62; foreign 41–2; language and 15; previous 42–7; situation and 25–6; social 23–31, 33
ephemera 83–4, 130
epics, primitive 56, 63
Erskine-Hill, Howard 162
etymology 161
events, 74–6; historical and literary 118
evidence: historical 73–7, 101 ff.; of senses 101–2
evolution, Darwinian 144
exemplification, principle of 54

fakes 58
fallacy, intentional 10, 153
Febvre, Lucien 108, 160
fiction: historical 88–9; science 46; serial 141–2
Fielding, Henry, 113; *Tom Jones* 52, 90–1
Fish, Stanley 147, 156, 166
foreknowledge, God's 157
formalism 5–6, 139
Frege, Gottlob 152
Freud, Sigmund 108, 165
Frye, Northrop 1–2, 7, 134–7, 159, 161, 164–5

Gadamer, Hans Georg 158
gardening 99
Garrick, David 52
Gide, André: *Les Caves du Vatican* 144–5
God: decline of faith in 144; Protestant experience of 37

INDEX

Goethe, J. W. von 124
Gombrich, E. H. 156, 157
Gower, John: *Confessio Amantis* 50
Graff, Gerald 163
Grahame, Kenneth: *The Wind in the Willows* 29
Greenblatt, Stephen 152, 158
Greene, Donald 121, 161
Greg, W. W. 95–6
Grice, H. P. 155
Gross, John 161
Guillory, John 164
Gumbrecht, H. U. 162

Hannibal 69
Harris, James 165
Harris, M. 161
Harris, Roy 153
Harvey, A. D. 162
Heidegger, Martin 146
Hexter, J. H. 160, 162
Heyer, Georgette 88
Hinman, Charlton 96
Hirsch, E. D., Jr 9–10, 11, 14, 152, 153, 155
historian, aims of 71, 72–7
historicism, new 158–9, 163
history: diachronic or synchronic 158; literary 7, deficiencies of 118–25; literature and 1
Hoban, Russell: *Riddley Walker* 156
Hogarth, William 102–3, 160
Hoggart, Richard 159
Holland, Norman 141, 142–3, 153, 165, 166
Holmes, Richard 159
Holmes, Sherlock 29
Homer 50; deities in 146; *Iliad* 50, 56, 61–2; *Odyssey* 50, 56
homoeopathy 126
Hood, Robin 29
hylozoism 19

idealism, Kantian 144, 145
ideas, history of 70, 82–3, 106–7
imagination, historical 86–91, 102–3
Inchbald, Elizabeth: *Lovers' Vows* 49–50, 156
indeterminacy, places of 140, 142
Index of Christian Art (Princeton) 160
inertness, law of increasing 55
information, history of 70–1
Ingarden, Roman 139–43, 159, 166

Innocent Adultery 85
instinct 157
intentions: God's 10, 153; authors' 10
interpretation: aims of 59–60; allegorical 57–8, 60; literary 9, 23; medieval *see* allegorical
inventory, social 104–6
Irigaray, Luce 165
Iser, Wolfgang 140–1

Jakobson, Roman 154
Jameson, Fredric 153, 163
Jauss, H. R. 161
Johnson, Barbara 166
Johnson, Samuel 50
Jones, Ernest 165
Joyce, James 4; *Ulysses* 4, 85
judgement 123
Juhl, P. D. 153
Jung, C. G. 165
justice, poetic 29

Kant, Immanuel 144, 163
Kean, Edmund 156
Keats, John 51; 'Ode on a Grecian Urn' 32
Keynes, J. M. 167
Klein, Melanie 165
knowledge: direct, 66–70, 71, 72, 157–8; defined 64; historical 6; indirect 66–71, 157, 158; defined 64, 65; of present 64; previous 67–71, 157, 158; anachronistic 72; defined 65–6; theory of 13
Kolodny, Annette 164
Krieger, Murray 165

Lacan, Jacques 165
Lamb, Charles 94
language 23; theory of 12–13, 143–4
Laocoon 37
Leavis, F. R. 7, 126–8, 131, 132, 162–3; followers of 133–4
Leibniz, Gottfried Wilhelm 117
Lentricchia, Frank 155
Levi, Primo: *If Not Now, When?* 158–9
Lévi-Strauss, Claude 138, 165, 166
libraries 100–1, 106, 110–12
Lichtenberg, G. C. 102–3, 160
Linnaeus, Carolus 99, 112, 159–60
literature: critics' 61; foreign 41–2; pastness of 37 ff.
Locke, John 123; *Essay* 82, 162

Lodge, David 165
London as setting 26–7, 29–30
Lord Aimworth 85
Lovejoy, A. O. 107, 121–3
Lukács, Georg 54, 156
McGann, J. J. 152, 155, 159, 161, 162
Mackenzie, Henry: *The Man of Feeling* 85
Marsh, Robert 165
Marvell, Andrew: 'To His Coy Mistress' 53, 54
meaning: apparent and latent 138; arriving at 16–21; changes in resisted 15–16; criterion of 9, 10, 21; indeterminate 32; significance vs 4; triangle of 11–12
memory 66–8
microforms 100–1, 110–11
Miller, J. H. 166
Milton, John 35–6, 50, 93, 97, 113, 114–15, 120, 156; *Paradise Lost* 44, 51–2, 75–7; sonnets 147
models, semantic 12
modernism 4
Moi, Toril 153
More, Sir Thomas: *Utopia* 46–7
Mozart, W. A.: *Don Giovanni* 137
Munz, Peter 158
Murdoch, Iris 49
museums 81, 104–6
music, free interpretations of 61
myths, cultural 28

Napoleon 75
Nelson, Horatio 38
Nietzsche, Friedrich 146
norms, literary 83
North, Sir Thomas 156
Norton Anthology 53
notes, explanatory 54

Oakeshott, Michael 157
objects, survival of 69
Oedipus 138
Ogden, C. K. 9, 13–14
O'Keeffe, John: *Wild Oats* 50
Olivier, Laurence 87
Olsen, S. H. 155
Ovid 85–6; *Metamorphoses* 57–8, 60, 62
Ovid moralisé 156

Pafford, J. H. P. 165
Parthenon 56–7, 60
past, knowledges of 6, 63–91

Patterson, Lee 152
Pearce, Roy Harvey 9
Pechter, Edward 163
Pepys, Samuel 51, 82–3
periods, literary 118–25
philosophy, history of 82
Picard, Raymond 61, 157
Plutarch 156
Poe, E. A.: *The Purloined Letter* 141, 142–3
poets, metaphysical 54
point of view: minority 126; philological and philosophical 12, 14
Pollard, A. W. 111
Pope, Alexander 50, 93, 115
Popper, K. R. 162
post-structuralism 143
Pound, Ezra 4
Pratt, M. L. 155
primitivism 82, 107
principle, co-operative 155
Propp, Vladimir 160
psychology, Freudian 141
Pushkin, A. S.: *Eugene Onegin* 155

Rabelais, François 113
Racine, Jean 61
Rawson, Claude 162
re-enactment 86–8
reading, living vs dead 53–4
Redgrave, G. R. 111
Rembrandt: *The Night Watch* 37
Richards, I. A. 9, 13–14, 139, 153
Richardson, Samuel 54; *Clarissa* 74
Richardson, Tony: *Tom Jones* 90–1
Robertson, D. W., Jr 2, 156, 166
romanticism 107, 121–5
Rosenbaum, S. P. 159
Round Table, Knights of 29
Russell, Bertrand 157
Ryan, Michael 161

St Paul's 56
St Peter's 56
Satan, Milton's 51–2
Saussure, F. de 13, 14, 154, 158
scepticism, moral consequence of 10
scholarship, individual vs co-operative 97–101
science: 98, 112; history of 82; hypotheses of 89
Scott, Sir Walter 88, 94, 156; *Heart of Midlothian* 44–7
Searle, John R. 9

semantics 12; literary 6
settings, physical 80–1
Seven Years War 74
Shakespeare, William 36, 38, 50, 63, 79, 95, 96, 114–15, 120, 129, 156; adaptations by 60; anachronistic performances of 87–8; audiences of 78; plays: *Coriolanus* 51, *Hamlet* 21–2, 23, 52, 55, 72, 76–7, 138, *Henry V* 87, *Henry VII* 51, *King John* 32, 52, *King Lear* 51, 59, 156, *Macbeth* 51, *The Merchant of Venice* 44, *Othello* 85, 97, *Twelfth Night* 50, *The Winter's Tale* 165; popularity of 51
Shelley, P. B. 51
Sheridan, R. B.: *The Rivals* 85–6
Showalter, Elaine 163, 164
Siddons, Sarah 51
Sidney, Sir Philip: *Arcadia* 49
significance vs meaning 4
situation 16–18, 23, 24, 25, 33
Smith, Henry Nash 164
Smollett, Tobias: *Peregrine Pickle* 85–6; *Roderick Random* 85–6
Southey, Robert 94
specialization: single-author 7, 109; single-genre 7, 92, 95–8
Spenser, Edmund 113
statements: indeterminate 20; meaningless 21
Steiner, Peter 155
Stephen, Leslie 153
Sterne, Laurence 113; *Tristram Shandy* 85
Stowe, H. B.: *Uncle Tom's Cabin* 156
strata 139
structuralism 7, 134, 137–9, 146, 165
Survey of London 80
Swift, Jonathan 50; *Gulliver's Travels* 15, 29, 40, 44, 46–7, 49

tabula rasa 87
Taine, Hippolyte 1, 13
Tate, Nahum 156
Tennyson, Alfred 51
text 23, 24, 25
theatre: actors' 61; directors 60–1
theory, expressive 34, 154
Thomas, D. M.: *The White Hotel* 158
Thorkelin, G. J. 37–8

Tompkins, J. P. 156
Tompkins, Jane 164
toothbrush, electric 19
triangles: of interpretation 6, 9–36, 54; of linguistic interpretation 16–17; of linguistic utterance 16–17; of literary interpretation 25
Trilling, Lionel 152

Ur-Hamlets 59
utopias 46–7
utterances 16–18, 25, 154; *see also* acts, speech

value, literary 4
Vaughan, Henry 4
Venus de Milo 37
Vico, Giambattista 1
Vinci, Leonardo da: *The Last Supper* 37
Virgil 50

Walsh, William 163
Warburg Institute (London) 160
Waterloo, Battle of 75–7, 159
Weinbrot, H. D. 162
Wellcome Museum (London) 106, 160
Wellek, René 121–4, 159, 162
Wellington, Duke of 75
Welty, Eudora; 'The Worn Path' 36
Whalley, George 162
Whole Duty of Man 85
Whorf, B. L. 154
Williams, Raymond 162
Williamsburg 81
Wimsatt, W. K. 153, 164
Wing, Donald 111
wit 123
Witherspoon and Warnke 53
Wittreich, J. A., Jr 156
Wodehouse, P. G. 137
Woodhouse, A. S. P. 2–3, 5, 152
Woolf, Virginia 157
Wordsworth, William 50, 93, 94, 125; *The Excursion* 51; 'The Idiot Boy' 21; *The Prelude* 51
Wrangham, Francis 94
Wright, Patrick 159

Zinnemann, Fred: *High Noon* 28

For Product Safety Concerns and Information please contact our EU representative GPSR@taylorandfrancis.com
Taylor & Francis Verlag GmbH, Kaufingerstraße 24, 80331 München, Germany